SOCRATIC PERPLEXITY

Socratic Perplexity

and the Nature of Philosophy

GARETH B. MATTHEWS

OXFORD

UNIVERSITY PRESS

OXFORD

UNIVERSITY PRESS

Great Clarendon Street, Oxford OX2 6DP

Oxford University Press is a department of the University of Oxford.
It furthers the University's objective of excellence in research, scholarship,
and education by publishing worldwide in

Oxford New York

Athens Auckland Bangkok Bogotá Buenos Aires Calcutta
Cape Town Chennai Dar es Salaam Delhi Florence Hong Kong Istanbul
Karachi Kuala Lumpur Madrid Melbourne Mexico City Mumbai
Nairobi Paris São Paulo Singapore Taipei Tokyo Toronto Warsaw

with associated companies in Berlin Ibadan

Oxford is a registered trade mark of Oxford University Press
in the UK and in certain other countries

Published in the United States
by Oxford University Press Inc., New York

British Library Cataloguing in Publication Data
Data available

Library of Congress Cataloging in Publication Data
Data available

ISBN 0–19–823828–2

1 3 5 7 9 10 8 6 4 2

Typeset by Hope Services (Abingdon) Ltd.
Printed in Great Britain
on acid-free paper by
Biddles Ltd,
Guildford & King's Lynn

For Rogers

ACKNOWLEDGEMENTS

THE idea for this book developed out of discussions in the Five-College Socrates Task Force, which met irregularly during the academic year, 1993–4, and included in its core membership Jyl Gentzler, Susan Levin, Heather Reid, and me. I began lecturing on Socratic perplexity in the summer of 1994, when I read a paper on its importance for education at a conference on thinking at MIT. I have read papers on Socratic perplexity in either Plato or Aristotle or both at the University of Vermont, the University of Wisconsin, meetings of the Society for Ancient Greek Philosophy, the University of Virginia, the University of Colorado, the University of Rostock, the University of Minnesota at Morris, the Pacific meetings of the American Philosophical Association, the Boston Area Colloquium in Ancient Philosophy, the City University of New York, Macalester College, Cambridge University, Boğaziçi University (Istanbul), and Haverford College. Although the various people at those lectures who through their comments and criticisms helped me clarify my thoughts on Socratic perplexity and the nature of philosophy are too many to mention, I thank them anyway.

The single individual who deserves the most thanks for helping me bring this book to its present form is my close friend and long-time collaborator, Marc Cohen. Thanks are also owed to Charles Kahn and to a second, anonymous, reader for Oxford University Press for their helpful criticisms and suggestions.

G.B.M.

Amherst
July 1998

CONTENTS

'Protagoras,' [Socrates] said, 'please don't think that I have any other wish in our discussion than to examine those things that I keep finding perplexing.'

Protagoras 348c5–7

I

Perplexity and the Figure of Socrates

No doubt some philosophers are much more given to perplexity
than others. Certainly some of us admit to being perplexed much
more readily than others do. Still, perplexity is so central to philosophy, to what interests us in philosophical questions in the first
place, and to what keeps us awake at night thinking about them, that
it is hard to imagine a good philosopher who is not thoroughly
familiar with the bewilderingly unsettling experience of being philosophically perplexed.

Take Descartes. He is not a philosopher who finds it easy to
acknowledge that he is perplexed. Whereas we speak of 'Socratic
perplexity', it is 'Cartesian doubt' we talk about, not 'Cartesian perplexity'. Descartes gives the clear impression that he likes to be in
charge of what he is doing. Certainly he puts himself in charge of
doubting. He even has a method for doing so, the 'Method of
Cartesian Doubt'. He uses doubt to search for the indubitable. Thus
he harnesses doubt to produce knowledge. But being perplexed is
very different from doubting. One is gripped by perplexity. One is
at its mercy. To be sure, perplexity can be a great motivator. But
one cannot command perplexity, the way Descartes commands
doubt.

Yet there are passages in which even Descartes shows that he is
perfectly well acquainted with the state of being perplexed. Thus,
after detailing in *Meditation* I the profoundly disturbing realization
that he might not, after all, be 'sitting by the fire, wearing a winter
dressing-gown', that he might instead be only dreaming that he is
doing those things, Descartes begins *Meditation* II with a striking, if
brief, expression of epistemological vertigo. 'It feels', he writes, 'as if
I have fallen unexpectedly into a deep whirlpool which tumbles me
around so that I can neither stand on the bottom nor swim up to the

top.'[1] This is the disorienting feeling of cognitive helplessness characteristic of philosophical perplexity.

Besides Descartes's question about how he can be certain he is not now dreaming there is a second dream question that can also induce philosophical perplexity, and not only in a famous philosopher either. At 6 years of age, Tim, while busily engaged in licking a pot, asked his father, 'Papa, how can we be sure that everything is not a dream?'[2]

I take Tim's question to be, like Descartes's, paradigmatically philosophical; it is also paradigmatically perplexing. Even though I have myself spent an inordinate amount of my life thinking about it, versions of it can still induce perplexity in me.

Plato puts the first dream question, the one Descartes raises in *Meditation* I, in the mouth of Socrates in this passage from his dialogue, *Theaetetus*:

There's a question you must often have heard people ask—the question what evidence we could offer if we were asked whether in the present instance, at this moment, we are asleep and dreaming all our thoughts, or awake and talking to each other in real life.   (158bc, Levett trans.)

This question and Tim's question are closely related, but they are not identical. Socrates does not, with his question, cast doubt on the very distinction between dreaming and waking life. Tim does, with his. Socrates asks what evidence we could offer that, at the present moment, we are in our waking phase, rather than our dreaming phase. Tim asks how we can be sure there even is such a thing as waking life. Descartes, in his *Meditations*, first asks Socrates' question; he moves on later to Tim's.[3]

Tim seems not to have languished long in the whirlpool of philosophical perplexity. He soon worked out an answer to his question that satisfied him, at least for the time being. 'Well, I don't think

---

[1]   *The Philosophical Writings of Descartes*, vol. ii, trans. Cottingham, Stoothoff, and Murdoch, (Cambridge: University Press, 1984), 16 (AT vii. 24).

[2]   Gareth B. Matthews, *Philosophy and the Young Child* (Cambridge, Mass.: Harvard University Press, 1980), 1.

[3]   See my *Thought's Ego in Augustine and Descartes* (Ithaca, NY: Cornell University Press, 1991), esp. chs. 5 and 6.

everything is a dream,' he told his father, ' 'cause in a dream people wouldn't go around asking if it was a dream.'[4]

Unfortunately we don't have any additional information on Tim's reasoning. We don't know whether his idea was that, if everything were a dream, we wouldn't even understand the contrast between dream life and waking life. Perhaps it was that; perhaps it was something quite different.

Both Socrates and his interlocutor, Theaetetus, do, however, expand on Socrates' ruminations about what evidence one could offer for thinking one is now awake. Theaetetus adds this especially important remark:

There is nothing to prevent us from thinking when we are asleep that we are having the very same discussion that we have just had. And when we dream that we are telling the story of a dream, there is an extraordinary likeness between the two experiences. (158c, Levett trans.)

Once we have Theaetetus' idea of telling a dream *in a dream*, it is but a short step to the thought that, for any test of whether one is awake—whether it be pinching oneself or something more sophisticated—it is conceivable that one might only be *dreaming* that one is giving oneself the test, and even dreaming that one is passing the test! (I shall have more to say on that issue in Chapter 11.)

Unlike Tim, Socrates offers no solution to his dream question, either in the *Theaetetus* or in any other of the Platonic dialogues. Although the argument from silence is weak, especially when one is interpreting a clever and artful philosopher like Plato, one is left to conclude that Plato simply did not know what to have Socrates say about this question. In his dialogue he lets Socrates simply move on to other issues.

I have already said that Tim's question (about knowing whether *all* life is a dream) is not exactly the same as Socrates' question in the *Theaetetus* (about evidence that one is *now* awake). But is Tim's question nevertheless an expression of *Socratic* perplexity? That question needs to be clarified. It could mean any one of the following:

---

[4] *Philosophy and the Young Child*, 23.

(1) Is Tim's question ever raised by Socrates in one of the Platonic dialogues?

(2) Is Tim's question one which the historical Socrates actually raised?

(3) Does Tim's question express perplexity of the sort the historical Socrates was likely to have expressed?

(4) Does Tim's question express perplexity of the sort that the figure of Socrates in one or more of the Platonic dialogues expresses?

The answer to question (1) is 'No.' Although there is a fascinating discussion of the distinction between dream life and waking life in book 9 of Plato's *Republic* (571b–572b), it does not raise Tim's question. Nor is there any other passage in the Platonic corpus in which Socrates, or any other Platonic character, raises it.

The answer to (2) is 'We simply have no way of knowing.' Plato is our best source for guessing what philosophical questions the historical Socrates might have raised. Since Plato is silent on this one, we draw a blank.

Question (3) is much trickier. It assumes that we have a pretty good way of getting at what questions the historical Socrates was *likely* to have expressed.

There is a conventional doctrine about Plato's dialogues, which, if acceptable, would help us here. W. K. C. Guthrie gave it a clear expression when he wrote, in volume iv of his *A History of Greek Philosophy*[5] that Plato, in his earliest dialogues, 'is imaginatively recalling, in form and substance, the conversations of his master without as yet adding to them any distinctive doctrines of his own'. If we accept this doctrine, we can treat some set of early dialogues as faithful records of the 'form and substance' of Socrates' philosophical conversations. Analysing those records we can frame a picture of the historical Socrates from which we can say whether it would be likely that the historical Socrates would have expressed the perplexity that lies behind Tim's question.

The conventional assumption Guthrie states so clearly has, of course, been called into question. Thus Charles Kahn writes, 'The

[5] (Cambridge: University Press, 1962–75), 67.

Socrates of the dialogues is an ambiguous figure, at once Plato's historical master and his literary puppet.'[6] Kahn's remark certainly holds for the figure of Socrates in Plato's middle and later dialogues; but it holds for the Socratic figure in the early dialogues as well.

In any case, I shall not be concerned in this book with questions like (3). Rather, I shall be interested in questions like (4). Thus it will be no part of my project to extract a portrait of the historical Socrates from the dialogues of Plato so as to be able to say what he found perplexing, or what his attitudes toward perplexity were. Everyone agrees that the picture we get of Socrates in the *middle* and *late* Platonic dialogues is almost certainly unfaithful in important respects to the actual person who was Plato's teacher. But perhaps the figure of Socrates we get in even the earliest dialogues is also unfaithful to history. We cannot know for sure. So, whereas speculation about questions like (3) is difficult to support and unlikely to convince the sceptics, we can say much more satisfactory things about questions like (4) and support them in a much more nearly adequate way. Here again, an admonition from Charles Kahn is pertinent. Where the portrait of Socrates in the writings of Plato is unfaithful, Kahn warns us,

we are in no position to correct it. As far as we are concerned, the Socrates of the dialogues *is* the historical Socrates. He is certainly the only one who counts for the history of philosophy.[7]

My aim in writing this book is, then, to say something worth while about *the figure of Socrates* as it is presented by Plato in his dialogues. In Chapter 3 I shall offer some speculations about what might first have moved the historical person, Socrates, to do philosophy. But my speculations should be taken for just that, speculations. It is not my aim in this book to try to bring the historical Socrates into clear focus. I would not know how to do that, certainly not in a way that would be likely to convince sceptics.

Perhaps I should admit that I find Terence Irwin's careful and balanced assessment of the evidence for distinguishing the historical Socrates from Plato, in the early chapters of his recent book, *Plato's*

---

[6] 'Did Plato Write Socratic Dialogues?', in Benson (1992), 35.
[7] Ibid. 46.

Ethics,[8] quite persuasive. Nevertheless, I am not inclined to think
that Irwin has settled the matter, and, since trying to mark off the
historical Socrates from Plato is peripheral to my concerns in this
book, I want to leave open the option that the figure of Socrates,
even in the *Apology* and the early aporetic dialogues, is, in important
part, a literary and philosophical invention of Plato.

My topic, then, is Socratic perplexity as it is represented in the
dialogues of Plato, early, middle, and late. I want to discuss the perplexity that the figure of Socrates in the dialogues of Plato both displays in himself and induces in others, and, in some surprising cases,
induces in others but fails to display himself!

Making, as I just did, the conventional distinction among early,
middle, and late Platonic dialogues, I inevitably raise contentious
questions about the order in which Plato wrote his dialogues. I also
invite consideration of the fascinating, but even more contentious,
issue about whether Plato's dialogues can or should be taken to
display a line of philosophical development. Most Platonic scholars,
at least in the recent literature, have thought they could trace a
course of philosophical development in Plato's writings. Yet
there have been distinguished commentators who are strongly antidevelopmentalist. Werner Jaeger declared boldly, 'When [Plato]
wrote the first words of his first Socratic dialogue, he knew the whole
of which it was to be a part.'[9] In any case, one might take either side
of the developmental dispute and remain agnostic or sceptical on the
issue of identifying the historical Socrates.

The debate between the 'developmental interpretation' of Plato's
dialogues and the 'unitarian interpretation', nicely summarized in
Charles Kahn's richly informed book, *Plato and the Socratic
Dialogue*,[10] has tended to focus on Plato's Theory of Forms. Thus
scholars have asked whether the Theory of Forms is already present in,
say the dialogue, *Euthyphro*, or if not the full-blown Platonic theory,
something we might identify as an earlier Socratic Theory of Forms.[11]

    [8] Irwin (1995).   [9] Jaeger (1944), 96.
    [10] Kahn (1996), 'Two Alternative Readings of the Dialogues', 38–42.
    [11] See, for example, Allen (1970), *Plato's 'Euthyphro' and the Earlier Theory of
Forms*. For a magisterial effort to distinguish Socratic Forms from Platonic Forms,
see Fine (1993), 'Socratic Forms', 49–54.

Since Plato's Theory of Forms is perhaps the boldest and most challenging metaphysical and epistemological theory in the history of philosophy, we naturally find it intriguing to think about how Plato might have arrived at it. There is, however, a way in which the connection between developmentalism and *perplexity* is even more interesting than that between developmentalism and the Theory of Forms. As I am going to suggest at the end of this book, many of us philosophers today can come to realize that the place perplexity occupies in our own philosophizing quite naturally goes through phases that seem to recapitulate the career of perplexity in the writings of Plato. It is therefore overwhelmingly natural to attribute to Plato himself shifts in attitude toward perplexity, and shifts in the role he is willing to assign to perplexity in philosophical inquiry. We cannot prove that the shifts we note in his writings mirror his own shifting attitudes and beliefs; but recognizing our own autobiographies foreshadowed in the progression of his writings, we very naturally suppose that his philosophical biography lies behind that progression and that it can function as an archetype for us.

Still, what I shall have to say in the following chapters should not be rejected automatically by even the most resolute Jaegerian antidevelopmentalist. Thus, although I shall mostly assume rather conventional ideas about the development of Plato's philosophy, the comparisons and contrasts I draw between the treatment Plato gives Socratic perplexity in this dialogue and that can easily be given a pedagogical, as well as a straightforwardly developmental account. Thus we can suppose, as I do, that Plato's own views about Socratic perplexity changed during his lifetime, or we can say that what he chose to display changed from dialogue to dialogue. We can at least *suspect* that variations in the perplexity he chose to display reflect changes in his own attitude toward perplexity; but we need not.

Thus, for example, I shall be interested in pointing out, in Chapter 5, that Socrates insists in a famous passage in the dialogue *Meno* that he is just as perplexed about the matter under discussion as his interlocutor is. In the *Republic*, by contrast, Socrates never avows or displays any perplexity whatsoever about any of the extremely perplexing matters under discussion. In part I of the dialogue *Parmenides*, however, a young Socrates becomes thoroughly perplexed about a variety of issues that concern Plato's Theory of Forms, the very theory that plays such an important role in the *Republic*. What is one to make of such shifts?

As a matter of fact, I take the *Meno* to be one of the last of the early Platonic dialogues, the *Republic* to be a middle dialogue, and the *Parmenides* to be either a late middle or early late dialogue. In Chapters 5 to 8 I will suggest a developmental story that might account for shifts in Plato's portrayal of Socratic perplexity from the *Meno* through the *Republic* to the *Parmenides*.[12]

Suppose now a reader protests, 'You have no right to assume that these differences in the portrayal of Socratic perplexity reflect shifts in Plato's own developing attitude toward philosophical perplexity. It could be, for all you or anyone else knows, that Plato himself was just as perplexed about the Theory of Forms when he wrote the *Republic* as he was when he wrote the *Parmenides*.'

To me, it is overwhelmingly natural to assume that Plato's own attitude toward perplexity shifted from the *Meno* to the *Republic* to the *Parmenides*. But I must agree with my imagined objector that we do not know, indeed, we cannot know, that my assumption is correct. What we do know is that the attitudes toward philosophical perplexity that the figure of Socrates expresses in Plato's dialogues shift from one dialogue to the other. We can interpret that shift as a direct expression of successive changes in Plato's own attitudes, or we can try to tell a more complex story about how the shift reflects changes in Plato's pedagogical aims. Thus it is conceivable that Plato, when he wrote the *Republic*, had already thought of all the reasons for being perplexed about the Theory of Forms that he presents in the *Parmenides*. He could have had pedagogical reasons for withholding those reasons until students had mastered the theory itself. Although in what follows I shall suggest the simpler hypothesis, I do not mean to rule out the more complex one.

Even though this book is about perplexity and the figure of Socrates in the dialogues of Plato, not every chapter is squarely on that topic. Chapter 2 is, in fact, about Aristotle and the Presocratics; Chapter 10 is about perplexity in the dialogue *Sophist*, in which the

---

[12] Cf. Bostock (1988), 13–14.

figure of Socrates takes a back seat; and Chapter 11 is, again, about Aristotle.

Aristotle, it turns out, is useful for framing my topic. He gives us suggestions about perplexity and the beginning of philosophy that lead naturally to Socrates. And the story of what happens to perplexity in Aristotle's own writings fills out and illuminates what will have been said earlier about perplexity and the figure of Socrates. As for Plato's dialogue *Sophist*, the way the Eleatic Stranger in that dialogue takes over from Socrates and pursues the dissolution of perplexity is also part of the story of perplexity and the figure of Socrates in the dialogues of Plato.

2

Perplexity and the Beginning of Philosophy

SOMEWHAT hidden away in Aristotle's treatise *On the Heavens* (*De caelo*) there is an interesting puzzle toward which Aristotle displays an intriguing ambivalence. On the one hand, he devotes a great deal of attention to it; in fact he discusses it for almost two of the fourteen chapters that make up book 2 of that work. On the other hand, he is rather apologetic in the way he introduces it, as if he were a little embarrassed to be bringing it up. This puzzle, he says at 294ᵃ10–11, must have occurred to everybody. Anyone who has not been astonished by it, he adds, rather sarcastically, must have quite an 'untroubled mind' (*alupoteras dianoias*).

Why is Aristotle so apologetic about bringing up this puzzle? He doesn't say. My own purely speculative hypothesis is that Aristotle remembers having thought about it himself as a child. Since Aristotle has a rather low regard for children, and for childhood—he says flatly that 'the life we lead as children is not desirable, for no one in his senses would consent to return again to this'[1]—such a memory from his own childhood would be reason enough for him to be at least a little embarrassed to be discussing this puzzle as an adult, especially in such a learned treatise.

Here is Aristotle's statement of the puzzle (call it 'the Stationary Earth Puzzle'):

... while a little bit of earth, let loose in mid-air, moves, and will not stay still, and the more there is of it the faster it moves, the whole Earth, free in mid-air, should show no movement at all. Yet here is this great weight of earth, and it is at rest. (294ᵃ13–17, Stocks trans.)

---

[1] *Eudemian Ethics*, bk. 1, ch. 5 (1215ᵇ22–4), trans. Solomon.

This puzzle, Aristotle goes on to say, has become a commonplace of philosophy (*philosophēma pasin*). Yet it is astonishing, he adds, that the various solutions that have been offered to it by earlier philosophers introduce greater absurdities than the absurdity of the original puzzle itself.

With that last comment Aristotle puts himself in position, not only to criticize his predecessors, but also to present with some air of triumph his own solution to the Stationary Earth Puzzle. Among the solutions Aristotle reviews, and rejects, there is one which, he tells us, is attributed to the very first Western philosopher, Thales:

Others say the Earth rests upon water. This, indeed, is the oldest theory that has been preserved, and is attributed to Thales of Miletus. [The Earth] was supposed to stay still because it floated like wood and other similar substances, which are so constituted as to rest upon water but not upon air. (294ª28–32, Stocks trans.)

Against this theory Aristotle poses two decisive objections. One objection is that, as a matter of empirical fact, earth simply does not float on water; it sinks in water. (More precisely, it dissolves and sinks at the same time.) As Aristotle puts the objection: 'If earth as a whole is capable of floating upon water, that must obviously be the case with any part of it. But observation shows that this is not the case' (294ᵇ3–4). What observation shows is that clods of earth actually *sink* in water.

The objection Aristotle mentions first is more general. The supposition that the Earth rests on water will not offer a satisfying explanation of why the Earth stays in place, he points out, unless we already understand why water stays in place (assuming, of course, that it does). One is reminded of the story about the woman who said that the Earth rests on the back of a giant tortoise. To the obvious question, what does the tortoise rest on, she replied, disarmingly, 'Don't worry, there are turtles all the way down!'[2]

---

[2] In some versions of the story it is an elephant that holds the world up and there are 'elephants all the way down'. Stephen Hawking tells a nice version of the story on p. 1 of his *A Brief History of Time* (New York: Bantam Books, 1988). Hawking tells the story as an exchange at an astronomy lecture, possibly one given by Bertrand Russell. Russell certainly knew the story (see, for example, his reference to an elephant-and-turtle version of the story in 'Reflections on My Eightieth Birthday', in his

Aristotle's own solution to the Stationary Earth Puzzle is characteristically ingenious. 'If it is the nature of earth, as observation shows, to move from any point to the centre,' Aristotle writes,

as [it is] of fire contrariwise to move from the centre to the extremity, it is impossible that any portion of earth should move away from the centre except by constraint . . . If then no portion of earth can move away from the centre [except by constraint], obviously still less can the Earth as a whole so move. For it is the nature of the whole to move to the point to which the part naturally moves. Since, then, it would require a force greater than itself to move it, it must needs stay at the centre. (296^{b}27–297^{a}2, Stocks trans.)

The argument is elegant

(1) Earth naturally moves toward the centre; that is,
(2) each portion of earth is such that, unless it is constrained by a force greater than its own natural force, it will move toward the centre;
(3) whatever is a natural motion of each part is a natural motion of the whole; therefore,
(4) the whole Earth, unless it is constrained by a force greater than its own natural force, will move toward the centre.

To get our desired conclusion, that the Earth stays at the centre, we need to add in the quite natural assumptions that (*a*) the whole Earth is already at the centre, that (*b*) the Earth is not constrained by a force greater than its own natural force, and that (*c*) if something is already located at the place toward which it naturally moves and it is not constrained, it will simply stay there.

We today will have serious worries about the idea that the universe has a centre at all, and therefore about the idea that portions of earth naturally move there. But, within Aristotle's assumptions, his solution is quite satisfying.

In a famous passage in book 1, chapter 2, of his *Metaphysics* Aristotle says that philosophy begins in wonder. 'For it is owing to their wonder (*thaumazein*)', he writes, 'that people both now begin,

Portraits from Memory (New York: Simon and Schuster, 1951), 54–5, but Russell scholars tell me he got the story from William James. In any case, the story has a long history. (See John Locke's *Essay Concerning Human Understanding*, bk. II, ch. 23, section 2.)

and first began, to philosophize (*philosophein*)' (982^{b}12–13). The casual reader might understand Aristotle to suppose that philosophy begins in something like Kant's awe at the starry heavens above and the moral law within. But a closer look at the passage reveals that the wonder Aristotle has in mind is astonishment over basic puzzles, or perplexities (*aporiai*). It is puzzles over the origin of the universe, and puzzles over such astronomical subjects as the ones he discusses in his treatise *On the Heavens*, that Aristotle mentions specifically in the *Metaphysics* passage. Astonishment over these puzzles, he says, is what first led people to philosophize and what continues to move them to do so.

Aristotle's comment that philosophy originates in astonishment over not knowing how to resolve basic puzzles fits well with my suggestion that Aristotle may well have reflected as a child on the puzzle over what keeps the Earth in place. He uses the same words for 'puzzle' (*aporia* and its cognates) and 'wonder' (*thaumazein* and its cognates) in the passage from *On the Heavens* (*De caelo*) on the Stationary Earth Puzzle as he does in the *Metaphysics* passage concerning the origin of philosophy. In fact, he uses 'wonder' or 'be astonished' cheekily in the *De caelo* passage when he comments, 'One may well be astonished (*thaumazein*) that the solutions offered are not seen to involve greater absurdities than the puzzle (*tēs aporias*) itself' (294^{a}20–1). It seems he expects the readers of this passage to be already familiar with his contention that philosophy begins in astonishment over not being able to resolve basic puzzles.

One might think my choice of the Stationary Earth Puzzle to illustrate Aristotle's thesis is a poor one, since Aristotle's own solution to this particular puzzle is not really philosophy, but only bad physics. I am not moved by that objection. In fact, I think his response is both genuine philosophy and also bad physics! It is genuine philosophy because it is an a priori solution to a conceptual difficulty. Let me elaborate.

One form of Aristotle's puzzle—it is a form of the puzzle I myself can remember thinking about as a child—could be captured in the question, 'What holds the Earth up?' My childhood assumption that there is such a thing as up and down in the universe—not relative to this or that orientation, but absolutely—is no doubt what is primarily problematic about the puzzle in this form. Modern physics and cosmology have rejected that idea. I'm somewhat intrigued to note, however, that just as I was writing a first draft of this chapter the *New York Times* reported in a front-page story evidence that space is not uniform in all directions, and, even if there is no absolute up or down to space, there may be directions distinguishable quite independently of the bodies that occupy space.[3]

In any case, without the idea of a cosmic up and down, not relative to the surface of the Earth but an up–down line of direction quite independent of the placement of heavenly bodies in space, the puzzle I had as a child could not arise. By contrast, Aristotle's version of the puzzle does not use the idea of up and down, but only the notions of motion and rest. The whole Earth, he thinks, is 'free' and at rest in 'mid-air'. His question, then, is why it should remain at rest when even a small part of earth, let go of in mid-air, will move (and the more of it there is, he says, the faster it will move!). To disarm Aristotle's own puzzle we should reject the absolute contrast between motion and rest.

What we would be left with, if we removed the assumption that the Earth is the reference point, would be a question about why, when we let go of, say, a clod of earth, it *seems* to move toward the Earth, whereas the Earth *seems* not to move at all. Of course, neither Aristotle nor his philosophic predecessors had any inkling of Newton's Law of Gravity to appeal to in answering questions about the relative motion of Earth and clod, though they did have the more general ideas of attraction and repulsion.

Even if I am right in thinking that Aristotle's solution to his puzzle is genuinely philosophical, it is surely not, one might protest, an example of philosophy at its very best, or even an example of Aristotle's philosophy at its very best. Does Aristotle also offer superior examples of philosophical responses to astonishment over conceptual puzzles?

The answer is clearly 'Yes.' One puzzle (he calls it an *aporia*) to which Aristotle gives extended and very sophisticated attention is this one from his *On Generation and Corruption*:

[3] ' "This Side (Don't Ask Which) Up" May Apply to the Universe, After all', by John Noble Wilford, *New York Times*, Fri. 18 Apr. 1997, A1 and A22.

Our new question too—viz. What is the cause of the unbroken continuity of coming-to-be?—is sufficiently perplexing (*aporian hikanēn*), if in fact what passes away vanishes into what is not and what is not is nothing . . . why has not the universe been used up long ago and vanished away—assuming of course that the material of all the several comings-to-be was finite? (318ᵃ13-19, Joachim trans.)

Let's call this 'the Puzzle of the Non-Vanishing Universe'. Given, as Aristotle says, a finite amount of material, and given, as he fails to say here, but assumes, an infinite amount of time, the universe would have been 'used up long ago and vanished away', provided that

(1) everything in the universe eventually passes away;
(2) all passing away is passing away into nothing; and
(3) nothing comes to be out of nothing.

Since Aristotle is talking about material things in this section, he naturally takes (1) for granted. (2) is, of course, the assumption he wants to reject. But it may be surprising that he doesn't even mention (3) until much later in the discussion.[4] Aristotle seems to find the principle, 'Nothing comes out of nothing' (often stated in Latin as *ex nihilo nihil fit*), so fundamental that it doesn't occur to him to question it here.

Aristotle's solution to the Puzzle of the Non-Vanishing Universe is that the passing-away of one thing is a coming-to-be of something else, just as the coming-to-be of one thing is a passing-away of something else (318ᵃ23-5). Coming to be and passing away are thus what we might call 'recycling operations'. Because of the 'recycling' character of substantial change, things can pass away endlessly, even though there is only a finite amount of material, without the world's vanishing or being used up.

The philosophical interest of Aristotle's solution to this puzzle lies mostly in the way he is able to make a defensible distinction between what he calls mere 'alteration' and what he considers 'substantial change'—where alteration is a change in the features some substantial thing has and substantial change is the coming into being or passing out of existence of some substantial thing. His account is not a success unless he can say, in a satisfactory way, what it is for

----

4 319ᵃ22 ff.

material things to come to be or pass away, without warranting the conclusion that such coming to be and passing away is really alteration in the underlying matter (which would then be the true subject of change).

The Milesians (Thales, Anaximander, Anaximenes) had presumably supposed that all change is alteration of the underlying 'stuff'. They differed only in what they took the underlying stuff to be. Thus Thales seems to have taken it to be water, Anaximenes took it to be air, and Anaximander thought it is the 'indefinite' (*apeiron*). To respond adequately to the Puzzle of the Non-Vanishing Universe without in effect becoming a Milesian, Aristotle needed to offer an account of substantial change that wouldn't reduce it to mere alteration of the underlying stuff of the universe.

So here is a puzzle we might easily be astonished we don't know how to deal with. To deal with it satisfactorily we will have to do some basic metaphysics. Moreover, it is quite plausible to think that much of the earliest Western philosophy did arise from astonishment over this puzzle and several of its close relatives. At any rate, that is the picture Aristotle gives us.

3

Getting Perplexed about the Virtues

SUPPOSE Aristotle is right about how philosophy got started in the ancient Greek world. Suppose philosophy did arise, historically, from astonishment over how difficult it is to deal with basic puzzles about the universe. Is that also, as Aristotle suggests it might be, the way individual philosophers come to do philosophy? Even if Aristotle's account fits the biographies of the very first Western philosophers, the Presocratic ones, does it also fit those of later philosophers? In particular, does it fit Socrates?

I expressed scepticism in Chapter 1 about being able to establish with confidence anything philosophically interesting concerning the historical Socrates, as distinct from the figure of Socrates in Plato's dialogues. So my question about Socrates becomes a question about the figure of Socrates in the Platonic dialogues. Does Plato present the figure of Socrates in a way that makes it plausible to think of him as coming to philosophy through the astonished recognition that there are puzzles about the universe he doesn't know how to resolve?

The autobiography Plato has Socrates recount in the middle dialogue *Phaedo*, at 96a–99d, does suggest something very much like the Aristotelian account. Socrates is there made to say that, although as a young man he was an enthusiast about 'natural science' (*peri phuseōs historian*) and wanted to know the causes of everything, he soon got tripped up over, for example, puzzles about what happens when something grows (96cd). One of his puzzles about growth, he suggests later on at 101b, is how something small, say, a small amount of rich food, can make anything large. The assumption that generates this puzzle—it is an important assumption in Plato's thought—is that causation is a process of passing something along. On this assumption, a rich meal could not make anyone large unless the meal were itself large, so that it could pass along its largeness.

A few lines later in the autobiography, at 96e–97a, Plato has Socrates express puzzlement over how two could be thought to be the result of putting one and one together. It seems to Socrates in the dialogue that two could hardly be such a result, since, unless the one and the other one were already two, they wouldn't be two when they were put together.

Aristophanes, in his satirical play *The Clouds*, also presents Socrates as an investigator of natural phenomena. And one of the charges against Socrates at his trial seems to have been that he 'busies himself studying things in the sky and below the earth' (*Apology* 19b). It is certainly plausible to think that many Athenians considered Socrates to be concerned with puzzles over the natural world in much the way that his philosophical predecessors were.

Yet Socrates in the *Apology* rejects this characterization of his interests. 'You have seen this yourselves in the comedy of Aristophanes', he tells the jury,

a Socrates swinging about there, saying he was walking on air and talking a lot of other nonsense about things of which I know nothing at all. I do not speak in contempt of such knowledge, if someone is wise in these things . . . but, gentlemen, I have no part in it . . . (19bc, Grube trans.)

So how, according to the picture of Socrates that Plato gives us in the early dialogues, including the *Apology*, might Socrates have come to philosophy?

Although Aristotle makes no claim in his *Metaphysics* about how it was that Socrates in particular became interested in philosophy, he does make two other claims about Socrates that are relevant to the figure of Socrates in the early dialogues. The first is that Socrates concerned himself with ethical questions to the neglect of the world of nature as a whole (987b1–2).[1] And the other is that Socrates, again according to Aristotle, fixed thought for the first time on definitions, or analyses (*peri horismōn*) (987b3–4). Even though Aristotle doesn't try to say how the urge to do philosophy arose specifically in Socrates, one could use his comments about Socrates' interest in ethics and his interest in definitions, or analyses, to adapt the story Aristotle had developed for the Presocratics, so that it might also

---

[1] For reasons to be sceptical about Aristotle's claim, see Nails (1995), 79–83.

apply to the Socrates of the early, definitional dialogues. The hypothesis would be that philosophy arose for Socrates in the astonished recognition that the attempt to offer definitions of basic ethical terms generates puzzles, or perplexities, that one doesn't know how to resolve.

This hypothesis, as it turns out, accords quite well with the picture Plato gives us of Socrates in several of his early dialogues. If, like most commentators, we take the early dialogues to be our best guide to the historical Socrates, we may even want to give credence to the idea that the historical Socrates came to philosophy by this route. But whether or not we make any surmises about the historical Socrates, we can see in the figure of Socrates how a thoughtful person might be led to philosophy, not only by the surprised recognition that there are puzzles about the universe we do not know how to solve, but also by the surprised recognition that there are puzzles about the virtues we do not know how to deal with.

To understand how this development might come about, let's take, as an example, the early dialogue *Laches*. This dialogue is a sustained effort to arrive at a satisfactory definitional analysis[2] of courage. It contains two profound expressions of perplexity. The first, at 194ab, is brought on by a line of questioning Socrates directs to the second of Laches' two attempts to say what courage is. And the second expression of perplexity occurs at the very end of the dialogue, where Socrates says, 'We are all equally in perplexity (*homoiōs en aporia*)' (200e).

What in the dialogue leads to these two expressions of perplexity? And especially, what leads Socrates to make his own avowal of perplexity at the very end of the dialogue?

The dialectic of the dialogue presents a conceptual vice in which Socrates traps, not only his interlocutors, but also himself. One jaw

---

[2] Most commentators describe Socrates as searching for 'definitions'. In the *Laches* the search might be said to be for a definition of 'courage'. But, of course, it is not the English word 'courage', that Socrates could be thought to have wanted to define. Was it the Greek word for courage, *andreia*? There are reasons to be uncomfortable about saying that Socrates wanted to define the Greek word for courage, as distinct from his wanting to analyse the concept of courage or bravery that that word expresses.

In this book I shall try to fudge the issues that these questions raise and speak, most of the time, about 'definitional analyses'.

of the vice is the truism that courage is only a single virtue, and therefore only one part of virtue as a whole. The other jaw is the surprising claim that, to the contrary, courage is the whole of virtue, not merely a part.

The truism hardly needs defending. Socrates introduces it by suggesting to Laches that, since investigating virtue as a whole would be too daunting a task, they should begin by looking into only a single part of virtue, namely, the individual virtue, courage (190cd). After Laches makes two unsuccessful attempts to say what courage is, Nicias tries his hand at the task (194c). In the midst of his conversation with Nicias, Socrates reminds him that what they are discussing, courage, is only one part of virtue. To underline this point he mentions two other virtues, temperance and justice, which he identifies as being, like courage, proper parts of virtue as a whole. At the end of the dialogue, where Socrates again makes the claim that courage is only a part of virtue, he adds piety to his list of individual virtues—each, apparently, distinct from each of the others and each distinct from virtue as a whole (199e). So much for the truism.

The surprising claim—the other jaw of the conceptual vice that Socrates tightens on himself and his friends—is the claim that courage is nothing less than the whole of virtue. 'The thing you are now talking about, Nicias,' Socrates says, 'would not be a part of virtue but rather the sum of virtue [or: virtue as a whole]' (199d). I want to examine the reasoning Socrates uses to support this surprising conclusion a little later. But first I want to make it seem a little less outlandish than one might first suppose it to be.

Consider an analogy. Suppose I am a chess strategist. I might say that chess strategy has two parts, defensive strategy and offensive strategy. Someone might protest that the distinction I am trying to offer is unreal. It is an essential part of good defensive strategy, my critic may insist, to anticipate the offensive strategy of one's opponent. One needs to be good at offensive strategy to do that. Moreover, my critic may continue, sometimes a good *offence* is the very best defence. Moreover, the critic might conclude, parallel considerations apply to offensive strategy: a good grasp of offensive strategy presupposes a good grasp of defensive strategy. So chess strategy is really one. Or, to put the point more paradoxically, defensive strategy is the whole of strategy—not by excluding offensive strategy as irrelevant, but by including it as an essential part of itself. For parallel reasons, offensive strategy is the whole of strategy.

Let's return now from chess strategy to the issue of virtue. Many people find the doctrine of the 'unity of the virtues', as it is called, quite unappealing. Before trying to make it a little less unappealing, let me say something about why it is important. If virtue is really one, there can be no such thing as a genuine moral dilemma. Of course there could be *apparent* moral dilemmas, that is, situations in which, say, what wisdom demands might *seem* to go against what courage demands. But such dilemmas would be merely apparent. That is, they would rest on a failure to understand fully one or both of the demands in question. Thus I might think that courage requires me to defend my position in the face of overwhelming enemy forces, even though wisdom demands that I retreat and regroup my forces for a later counter-attack. But if virtue is really one, I am simply mistaken about at least one, if not both, of those requirements. Either what virtue requires is some quite different course of action, perhaps one I have not yet considered, or else I am simply wrong about what courage demands, or else wrong about what wisdom demands. Since many people have thought that they and others sometimes face genuine moral dilemmas, the doctrine of the unity of virtue is, if acceptable, a significant corrective to this widespread belief.

There is a modern point of view from which the unity of virtue does make perfect sense; it is the viewpoint of utilitarianism. According to the simplest form of utilitarianism, act utilitarianism, I should simply calculate the utility (where utility might be, say, the balance of pleasure over pain) that would be produced by each of the alternatives open to me when I face a moral decision. If standing my ground would produce more utility than any other alternative, then standing my ground is my duty in that situation. If retreating and eventually regrouping would produce more utility, then retreating is my duty in that situation. If the utility produced by these two alternatives is equal, and unsurpassed by any other alternative open to me, then I have a duty to take *one or the other* of these two courses of action, but I have no duty to take one *rather* than the other. Thus there can be no moral dilemma.

Neither Socrates, nor either of his chief interlocutors in the dialogue *Laches* is a utilitarian. But one of the interlocutors, Nicias, gives Socrates the materials for developing an argument for the unity of virtue which, like the utilitarian argument I have just sketched, would rule out the possibility of moral dilemmas. Building on a suggestion he claims to have taken from Socrates (194d), Nicias proposes that courage is a sort of wisdom (*poia sophia*) (194e). It is, he says, the sort of wisdom that has to do with what is to be feared and what is to be hoped for (194e–195a).

To get clear about what Nicias has in mind, consider again the battle situation I just mentioned. As I decide whether to stand my ground against overwhelming odds, what I fear most may be a painful death. Or it may be the humiliation of an ignominious retreat. I should estimate the chances of dying painfully and the possibilities of retreating, even if ignominiously. What I might most reasonably hope for under the circumstances may be salvaging my honour, or perhaps even achieving a certain nobility. Knowing how to rank these anticipated goods and feared evils, both with respect to their comparative importance and with regard to the likelihood that my actions might actually bring them about, and then acting appropriately on the basis of my knowledge,[3] is presumably the sort of thing Nicias wants to understand as courage.

In criticizing Nicias' suggestion, Socrates points out that knowledge of such goods and evils as I have just mentioned, including their importance and likelihood, is not a time-bound affair; in particular, it is not restricted to *future* goods and evils. If one has knowledge about goods and evils, that knowledge will include knowledge of past and present goods and evils as well. 'There is not one kind of knowledge by which we know how things have happened in the past, and another by which we know how they are happening at the present time, and still another by which we know how what has not yet happened might best come to be in the future,' he says; 'the knowledge is the same in each case' (198d). Thus there is no knowing about future goods and evils that does not include knowing about goods and evils *simpliciter*, which, he adds, is the sum of virtue (199e). And thus, if

---

[3] The assumption in the dialogue seems to be that one will act on one's knowledge.

Nicias is right in thinking that courage is the knowledge of what is to be feared and what is to be hoped for, it is not just a part of virtue but rather the whole of virtue.

As I have already mentioned, Socrates' strategy in this dialogue is to put himself and his interlocutors into a conceptual vice, one jaw of which is this rather surprising claim that courage is the whole of virtue. Suppose one were convinced by Socrates' reasoning in support of the surprising claim. Suppose one were inclined to agree that courage is, indeed, the whole of virtue. Wouldn't one then reject what I have described as the 'truism' that courage, being only a single virtue, is only a part of virtue as a whole? It seems that one should. Why then does Socrates not go back and reject this 'truism'? Why does he hold onto this other jaw of his conceptual vice and pronounce himself gripped, like his interlocutors, by perplexity?

Perhaps he holds onto the truism just because it is a truism. It is certainly a commonplace of Plato's dialogues that the virtues are many, and that among them are courage, temperance, justice, and piety. Beyond that, the earlier discussion suggests that both Socrates and his interlocutors find it plausible to accord a certain independence to courage, as over against wisdom, which is, of course, also a virtue. On the issue of independence consider, especially, the discussion of Laches' second definitional analysis, according to which courage was supposed to be wise endurance, that is, endurance (*karteria*) with practical wisdom (*meta phronēseōs*) (192c).

Socrates' way of testing such suggested definitional analyses is to search for counter-examples to them. If he can think of an example that his interlocutor is inclined to agree is a case of courage, even though the case fails to fit the definition, then the definition will have been shown to be too narrow. On the other hand, if he can think of an example that fits the definition but that his interlocutor is inclined to agree is not a case of courage at all, then the definition will have been shown to be too broad.

That's at least the way the simple counter-examples work. But sometimes Socrates' counter-examples are logically a bit more complicated. In fact, the most interesting counter-examples Socrates comes up with in the *Laches* to test the suggestion that courage is wise endurance concern, not the one-place predicate, '. . . is brave', but rather its two-place comparative form, '. . . is braver than . . .'. Thus Socrates considers a warrior whose endurance in battle is based on the shrewd calculation that reinforcements will soon give his side a great numerical advantage over the enemy. He contrasts this soldier with a warrior in the opposing camp who endures without any hope that his side will be similarly reinforced. Although the endurance of the first soldier is practically wiser than that of the second—as Laches agrees—it seems to be the endurance of the second soldier that is braver—as Laches also agrees. So, it seems, courage cannot be wise endurance. Unwise, or less wise, endurance may make one, it seems, more courageous than (merely) wise endurance.

Socrates follows up this counter-example with two more that make a similar point. One is the comparison between a horseman in a cavalry attack with knowledge of horsemanship and a horseman who lacks such 'know-how'. Laches acknowledges, what seems to be correct, that the cavalryman without the knowledge might well be braver (certainly the battle would be a great deal more frightening to him), so that again wiser endurance loses out in the bravery contest to less wise endurance.

The final counter-example is a comparison between divers who dive into wells, where the less skilled, and so less wise, are agreed by Laches to show more courage than the more skilled. The idea is presumably that, in a competition for bravery, knowing about how, where, and when to dive safely into a dark and threatening well makes the achievement of diving less frightening, and therefore less demanding in courage than knowledgeable diving.

Should Laches have agreed that, in the cases of these last three comparative judgements, the braver person is really the less knowledgeable one? I think so. Surely it does require more courage to stand by your post in the face of a massive attack without the knowledge that reinforcements are on the way. It also requires more courage for an unskilled horseman to take part in a cavalry attack than for a skilled one to do so. And it also requires more courage for an unskilled and inexperienced well-diver to dive into a well than for a knowledgeable one to do so. Of course, wisdom might require, in all three cases, that one not go through with the assignment. But suppose one ignored wisdom and went ahead anyway.

More bravery would be required in the case in which one lacked knowledge of reinforcements, or knowledge of horsemanship, or skill at diving into wells than would be required if one had the relevant knowledge.

If courage does indeed have the independence from wisdom that these counter-examples suggest, then we have additional reason to stick by the truism that courage is only one part of virtue. Perhaps one should give up on trying to be courageous in these cases of insufficient knowledge. But so long as there is the possibility of being braver than x even when one is clearly less wise than x, in fact, precisely *because of the fact* that one lacks relevant knowledge that x has in this situation, then, it seems clear that courage cannot be, by itself, the whole of virtue.

There is every reason to think of Socrates as being entirely candid when, at the end of the *Laches*, he says that he is just as perplexed as his interlocutors about courage and its relation to virtue as a whole. If he had not been, he would surely have shown how the seemingly independent pull of courage in these three cases I have mentioned is illusory or wrong-headed. Moreover, he would have denied the assumption he began with, that courage is only a part of virtue rather than the sum of virtue. Yet instead of denying the assumption, he repeats it at the end of the dialogue (199e).

Recent commentators have tried to determine whether Socrates himself accepted a strong version of the doctrine of the unity of the virtues, according to which the several virtues really are all *the same thing*, or only a weaker version, according to which a person can't have one virtue without having each of the others. These commentators have also argued among themselves about what clues, if any, we readers are meant to get concerning Socrates' real views on these matters from the dialogue *Laches*.

Gregory Vlastos tells us that Plato has good reason 'to discredit Nicias as a spokesman for Socratic knowledge . . .'.[4] He sees Plato as wanting 'to expose Nicias' incapacity to steer the Socratic definition through the rough waters of the terminal elenchus . . .'.[5] He does not take seriously the possibility that Socrates might have been himself

---

[4] Vlastos (1981), 268. [5] Ibid. 269.

perplexed, let alone that there might be something inherently perplexing about courage and its relation to the other virtues.
Terry Penner, whose pioneering article on the unity of the virtues[6]
instigated much of the recent discussion, sees the *Laches* this way:

> The prime exegetical question about the *Laches* is thus: What is Socrates up
> to in refuting an account of courage [namely, that it is the science of the fear-
> ful and the hopeful] that he should himself accept? Put in another way, what
> is Nicias, the proponent of this Socratic account of courage, missing, that
> leads to his refutation? Or better, what does Socrates want us to see Nicias
> as missing?[7]

On Penner's reading of the *Laches* the argument in that dialogue is
a reduction to absurdity of the claim that courage is only a part of
virtue.[8] To the objection that Socrates does not, in the dialogue,
draw any such conclusion, but says, even at the end, that he remains
perplexed, Penner has responses like this:

> Always assume that in refuting an interlocutor, Socrates has clearly in mind
> some point he wishes us to see even when his interlocutor does not himself
> see the point. In other words, never use Socratic ignorance as an argument
> against saying that Socrates has a view as to what has gone wrong when an
> interlocutor has been reduced to *aporia*.[9]

Yet, as I have been emphasizing, it is not just Socrates' interlocutors in the *Laches* who have been reduced to absurdity; it is also
Socrates himself. 'We are all equally in perplexity (*homoiōs gar en
aporia egenometha*)', he says.
My reading of the dialogue seems to accord with what Terence
Irwin says in his recent book, *Plato's Ethics*. 'In the *Laches* as in the
Charmides,' Irwin writes, 'an apparently cogent argument about
bravery has challenged the common-sense belief that one virtue is
distinct from all the others.' He adds: 'Socrates regards this as a genuine puzzle . . .'.[10]

---

[6] Penner (1973).   [7] Penner (1992a), 1.   [8] Ibid. 6.
[9] Ibid. 26. Again, 'wherever a dialogue leaves us in *aporia*, experience has suggested to me that the strategy of . . . assuming that there is something Socrates wants
us to see and trying to track it down . . . almost always pays dividends' ((1992b),
145–6).
[10] Irwin (1995), 44.

If we take Socrates at his word in this dialogue, then, he is indeed astonished to recognize that there is a perplexity about courage, and, implicitly, about each of the other virtues, that he doesn't know how to resolve. Each virtue seems to be quite distinct, in that one wouldn't normally think one had to discuss justice or temperance or piety in an effort to explain what courage is. Whether or not we today find Socrates' own reasoning persuasive for saying that courage is the whole of virtue, we may find attractive other reasons for concluding that there can be no genuine moral dilemmas, including dilemmas that pit courage against some other virtue, say, wisdom. If so, we should also find ourselves perplexed at the evidence that an individual virtue, such as courage (or honesty, or compassion), may seem to have some independent claim on us that resists full integration into the other demands of morality.

Reading the *Laches* the way I have suggested, we can find in it some confirmation of the hypothesis we had cobbled together from remarks in Aristotle that for Socrates, at least as he is portrayed in the early definitional dialogues, philosophy begins in the astonished recognition that he is not able to solve some basic puzzle[11]—perhaps not a puzzle about the cosmos, but rather a puzzle about ethics, and in particular, a puzzle about how to develop satisfactory definitional analyses of one of the individual virtues in a way that captures correctly its relation to virtue as a whole.

There is, however, an important way in which Aristotle's account in *Metaphysics*, book I of the genesis of philosophy fails to fit exactly the picture of Socrates in Plato's dialogue *Laches*. Aristotle uses the Greek word, *aporia*, variously translated 'puzzle', 'problem', 'difficulty', and 'perplexity', for identifiable conundrums, or puzzles. Following that usage, I have looked for, and found, in the *Laches* a relevant conundrum, or puzzle, about the relation between courage and the whole of virtue. But the conundrum I have isolated is not itself identified by Plato in this dialogue as an *aporia*, a perplexity.

---

[11] Robin Smith makes a similar connection between Aristotle and Socrates. 'Like Socrates,' he writes, 'Aristotle thinks that the first step in acquiring philosophical wisdom is the realization that our received wisdom is flawed, that there are puzzles and problems implicit in what we took to be most familiar and obvious. Philosophy begins with this puzzlement . . .' (Smith (1997), p. xviii).

Instead, Plato in this and other early dialogues tends to use *aporia* and its cognates for a state of mental confusion, bewilderment, or helplessness—the condition, to use Wittgenstein's phrase, of 'not knowing one's way about'.[12]

The word *aporia* has an interesting history in classical Greek. It is derived from *aporos*, which means 'without a means of passing a river', or, more generally, 'having no way in, out, or through'. Thus the first meaning of *aporia* in Liddell and Scott's *Greek–English Lexicon*[13] is 'difficulty of passing'. The word then comes to mean 'being at a loss, embarrassment, perplexity'. It is this meaning of *aporia* that is relevant to the text of the *Laches*. Later on, as Liddell and Scott point out, the word comes to mean 'question for discussion, difficulty, puzzle'. This is the sense Aristotle usually gives it in his writings.

I shall be arguing in a later chapter that this last shift in the meaning of *aporia* through Plato's writing into Aristotle goes along with a significant change in the methodological role they assign to perplexity. As for the *Laches*, what gets called *aporia* in that and other early and middle dialogues is the state of bewilderment that puzzles of a certain sort naturally induce. It is what Aristotle calls the state of being astonished (*thaumazein*) that one doesn't know how to resolve these puzzles.

As I have been arguing in this chapter, the puzzle that gives rise to the state of perplexity in the dialogue *Laches* is an ethical one that concerns how we are to understand courage and its relation to virtue as a whole. The *Laches* puzzle is a difficulty that should engage anyone who has ever worried about whether there can be any such thing as a genuine moral dilemma.

---

[12] 'A philosophical problem has the form: "I don't know my way about (*Ich kenne mich nicht aus*)" ', *Philosophical Investigations* (Oxford: Blackwell, 1967), 123.

[13] (Oxford: Clarendon Press, 1985), 215.

4

Getting Perplexed about Divine Normativity

THE early dialogue *Euthyphro* is similar, in several important ways, to the *Laches*. Both are definitional dialogues. And both end in apparent failure; they therefore count as 'aporetic dialogues', that is, dialogues that end in *aporia*, perplexity. To be sure, the word *aporia* does not actually occur in the *Euthyphro* (though, as we noted in the last chapter, both it and its cognates occur several times in the *Laches*). Nevertheless, Socrates' interlocutor, Euthyphro, gives us a nice display of philosophical perplexity when, after the crucial central argument, he erupts in frustration, 'But Socrates, I am simply unable to tell you what I think, for whatever we put forward goes around and refuses to stay put where we place it' (11b).

Socrates picks up on Euthyphro's expression of perplexity and embellishes it. In a welcome respite from the complex and abstruse reasoning that had gone on just before, he develops an analogy between himself and his ancestor, the sculptor Daedalus. Daedalus was said to have produced statues with so much movement that they were in danger of running away. Socrates allows that he, by his questioning, makes Euthyphro's statements slip and slide and refuse to stay put. Euthyphro eagerly accepts the Daedalus analogy and even underlines the point that it is Socrates, not he, who makes his statements go around in circles. So here, in this pause between two serious and conceptually demanding efforts to pin down the nature of piety, we have somewhat light-hearted reflections on the phenomenon of philosophical perplexity, on what may give rise to it and on the effects it can be expected to have.

One respect in which the *Euthyphro* differs from the *Laches* is in the number of its characters. Whereas the *Laches* is a conversation between Socrates and four other principal characters, Socrates in the *Euthyphro* has but a single conversation partner. Though Euthyphro, in the dialogue, comes across as an intelligent conversationalist, he expresses little eagerness for philosophical reflection. He seems to represent a person of strong convictions who is reluctant to admit the possibility that the conceptual underpinnings for his confident judgements need to be examined philosophically.

This dialogue begins as Socrates meets Euthyphro, who is on his way to a lawcourt to charge his father with impiety. Since the father's alleged offence is negligent homicide, the crime would presumably be thought an offence against the gods on the assumption that the gods would condemn such disregard for the value, perhaps even the sanctity or holiness, of human life.

Charging one's own father with a capital offence is, of course, a serious matter in any society, certainly in ancient Greek society. Euthyphro can be expected to have thought long and hard before taking this step. 'Then you must know what piety is,' says Socrates, slyly, and they are immediately off on a definitional search for what piety, or holiness (*to hosion*), is.

Socrates exposes several flaws in Euthyphro's early attempts to say what piety is. But the central conundrum of the dialogue arises from Euthyphro's suggestion that the pious is what the gods love and the impious is what they hate. In its fully qualified form, Euthyphro's suggestion is that the pious is what *all* the gods love, and the impious, what they *all* hate (9e). The qualification, 'all', is introduced to eliminate from consideration the cases in which the gods differ among themselves on what they love and what they hate.

Socrates responds to Euthyphro's suggested definition of 'piety' with the most famous line from the dialogue, indeed, one of the most famous lines in Plato, namely, the question, 'Is the pious loved by the gods because it is pious, or is it pious because they love it?' (10a). This conundrum, sometimes called 'the Euthyphro Problem', is Socrates' response to Euthyphro's attempt to understand divine preference or approbation as the defining characteristic of piety. But, as we shall see, the problem the question raises can easily be generalized. Very close relatives of Socrates' conundrum threaten any attempt to provide an essentially theological basis for normative judgements of human conduct. (Even more generally, the conundrum seems to pose a problem for understanding how the rulings of any authority can be both rationally based and decisively authoritative.)

Suppose we take as our sample act of piety the giving up of a burnt offering in thanksgiving for a victory on the battlefield. Suppose further that the gods do, in fact, love, or approve of, this action in this particular circumstance. We can now ask, 'But why do the gods love, or approve of, this action?' A correct, but only minimally informative answer might be 'They love it because it is pious, or holy.' But what is there about this action, we may still want to know, that *makes* it pious? Here is where the definitional analysis of the pious should come into play. If the suggested definition of 'pious', namely, 'loved by the gods', were satisfactory, that is, if it did actually succeed in capturing precisely that feature of pious actions that makes them pious, then we should be able to substitute the *definiens* for the *definiendum* and get a more informative explanation for why the action in question is pious.[1]

Such a substitution, however, produces, in this case, a troubling result. Substituting 'loved by the gods' for 'pious' in 'The gods love it because it is pious' we get: 'The gods love it because it is loved by the gods.' This result is a little like saying 'She loves her husband because she loves him.' Or: 'I like pickles [just] because I like them.' It does suggest, perhaps appropriately, that divine favour is the bottom line. But it also suggests, and this is the worrying part, that the gods need have no *reason* for loving one thing in preference to all alternatives.

Suppose the gods did have a reason for loving burnt offerings in thanksgiving for a military victory. Suppose that their reason were this: Such an action shows appropriate gratitude for divine favour. Then, it seems, showing appropriate gratitude for divine favour should figure essentially in any informative statement of what *makes* the offering a pious action. The more general idea might then be that performing pious actions is doing things that express an appropriate

---

[1] S. Marc Cohen, in his classic article, Cohen (1971*a*), suggests as a justifying principle for this move the rule that definitional equivalents are substitutable *salva veritate*. Richard Sharvy, in Sharvy (1972), suggests a more restricted principle, one which licenses the substitution of *definiens* for *definiendum* in certain 'because' contexts.

attitude towards the gods, or that foster a right relationship with them, by, for example, expressing gratitude for divine favours. But, if that were right, then 'pious' should not be *defined* as 'loved by the gods,' but rather as 'expressing appropriate attitudes towards the gods and fostering a right relationship with them', or something of the sort.

As a little reflection should make clear, the Euthyphro Problem is not just a problem about making sense of religious practices in ancient Greece, or even about understanding polytheism more generally. It is equally a problem for monotheistic religions like Judaism, Christianity, and Islam. Any thoughtful person who takes 'right' and 'wrong,' or 'just' and 'unjust,' or 'morally good' and 'morally bad' to *mean* 'commanded by God'/'prohibited by God', or 'approved by God'/'disapproved by God' must figure out how to deal with this puzzle. For on such an assumption it seems that the nature of any given action under consideration, whether an evil action like murder, or blasphemy, or a good action like self-sacrificial service to others, or mercy towards an offender, plays no *essential* role in determining its moral status. What counts is only whether it is, so to speak, on the list of divinely approved actions, or, alternatively, on the list of divinely disapproved actions.

If, on the other hand, we suppose that God has good reasons for commanding some actions (say, feeding the hungry) and prohibiting others (say, torturing small children) it must be because God can recognize the moral (or immoral) nature of these actions. But then, it seems, any satisfactory definition of 'right'/'wrong', 'just'/'unjust', or 'morally good'/'morally bad' should make appropriate appeal to the moral nature of morally good acts and to the immoral nature of morally bad ones, which natures would then be the rational basis for God's commandments and prohibitions.

The argumentation in the *Euthyphro* that leads up to the conclusion (at 10e–11b) that the pious and the god-loved are not the same thing is admittedly somewhat difficult to follow.[2] Yet the point of it is easy to appreciate. 'I'm afraid, Euthyphro,' says Socrates,

---

[2] In my judgement, the best guide through its intricacies is Cohen (1971*a*), although the interested reader will also want to consult Sharvy (1972), Geach (1966), and McPherran (1985).

that when you were asked what piety is, you did not wish to make its nature (*ousia*) clear to me, but you told me an affect or quality (*pathos*) of it, that the pious has the quality of being loved by all the gods, but you have not yet told me what the pious is.   (11ab, Grube trans.)

Suppose we tried responding to Socrates' criticism by saying that the nature (*ousia*) of the pious is just divine approval or love, and nothing else, and that that divine approval or love is precisely what makes pious acts pious. Clearly Socrates would be dissatisfied. And the reason he would be dissatisfied is that we would have made no allowance for a nature that the gods themselves could recognize, and, on the basis of that recognition, reward. The love and approval of the gods might be based on nothing more than merely whimsical preference.

I have already mentioned that the argument for the conclusion that the god-loved cannot be the same as the pious comes about halfway through the dialogue *Euthyphro*. What about the rest of the dialogue? Does it offer a satisfactory account of the nature of piety?

The conclusion to the dialogue suggests that the efforts of the last section to say what piety is are also unsuccessful. Thus, near the end of the dialogue Socrates announces, 'So we must investigate again from the beginning what piety is, as I shall not willingly give up before I learn this' (15c). Euthyphro responds, 'Some other time, Socrates, for I am in a hurry now, and it is time for me to go' (15e). In this ending we seem to have ample basis for thinking that the *Euthyphro* is an aporetic dialogue.

Yet some commentators have staunchly resisted that conclusion. Gregory Vlastos, the dean of American Socratic scholars, finds suggestions of a positive account of piety in the last section of the *Euthyphro*. In chapter 5 of his book, *Socrates: Ironist and Moral Philosopher*,[3] Vlastos puts the *Apology* together with the *Euthyphro* to flesh out that positive account.

What, then, does Vlastos see as the answer to the definitional question the *Euthyphro* is inching towards, but never quite reaching? He notes that, in the final effort to say what the nature of piety is, Euthyphro suggests 'service to the gods'. Vlastos also notes that

---

[3] Vlastos (1991).

Socrates rejects the idea of 'swapping gifts of sacrifice for prayed-for benefits'. This won't do because, writes Vlastos,

the gods stand in no need of gifts from us, while we are totally dependent on their gifts to us—'There is no good in our life which does not come from them' (*Euthyphro* 15a)—so we would be the exclusively advantaged party; if piety is holy barter it is a bargain for us, a swindle for the gods.[4]

Vlastos thinks, however, that Socrates has available to him a more sophisticated understanding of what 'service to the gods' might mean. He sees the 'critical point in the search' for a definitional analysis of piety in this Socratic question: 'In the performance of what work (*ergon*) does our service to the gods assist them?' (13e).

Vlastos then asks us to imagine that 'Euthyphro had been allowed a preview of the speech Socrates was to give at his own trial', a speech recorded in Plato's *Apology*. (It is important to keep in mind that the dramatic date of the action portrayed in the *Euthyphro* precedes Socrates' trial, which is recorded in the *Apology*, even though the *Apology* seems to have been written by Plato well before he wrote the *Euthyphro*.) In the speech from the *Apology* that Vlastos refers to, Socrates assures the judges, 'I believe that no greater good has ever come to you in the city than this service of mine to the gods' (*Apology* 30a). Vlastos goes on:

To derive from this a definition of piety Euthyphro would then have had to generalize, contriving a formula that would apply not only in Socrates' case but in every possible case of pious conduct. This is a tall order and it is by no means clear that Socrates himself would have been able to fill it. But this technical failure would not shake—would scarcely touch—the central insight into the nature of piety with which, I submit, we can credit Socrates on the strength of what Plato puts into his mouth in the *Apology* and the *Euthyphro*. *Piety is doing god's work to benefit human beings*—work such as Socrates' kind of god would wish done on his behalf in service to him.[5]

Can this be right?

I do not myself see how one can take the dialogue *Euthyphro* to heart and find Vlastos's suggestion satisfying. Surely the reader of this dialogue who listens to Vlastos's proposal will ask, indeed

---

[4] Vlastos (1991), 174.   [5] Ibid. 175–6.

should ask, the *Euthyphro* question, 'But is this service that, as you put it, "Socrates' kind of god wishes done in service to him" pious because god wishes it done on his behalf, in service to him, or does god wish it done on his behalf, in service to him, because it is pious?' To someone who accepts the first horn of this dilemma, Socrates can be expected to insist that the characteristic of God's wishing something to be done on his behalf can be at most a *pathos*, an incidental feature of pious actions, not their nature (*ousia*). And to the person who accepts the second horn, Socrates can protest that he still hasn't been told what makes such work pious and therefore hasn't been given any account of what the nature of piety is.

I do not contest Vlastos's suggestion that there are materials in Plato's *Apology* that might be used to try to fill out an account of what piety is. One might, for example, use the famous line from Socrates' penultimate speech, 'The unexamined life is not worth living' (38a). Piety might be taken to consist in, or at least to include, relentless examination of life, including, perhaps, examination of one's own life. Socrates' god, perhaps thinking that the philosophical examination of a life shows reverence for the value of life might wish us to examine our lives and the lives of others as an act of reverence. But then, of course, it would not be the divine wish that made this examination pious, but rather, say, the fact that it expresses an appropriate reverence for the value of human life.

A different tack is taken by C. C. W. Taylor in his article, 'The End of the *Euthyphro*'. Taylor notes that, even though dialogues like the *Euthyphro* end in *aporia*, it is 'not unknown for them to contain fairly clear hints of a conclusion which is not explicitly drawn'.[6] To flesh out the conclusion he believes is hinted at, though not explicitly drawn in the *Euthyphro*, Taylor appeals to other Platonic dialogues, specifically to the *Laches*, the *Charmides*, and the *Protagoras*, as well as to Aristotle's *Nicomachean Ethics*.

The answer that Taylor pieces together from these various sources is that piety is, in a certain way, identical with virtue, but it is virtue under its theological aspect. The idea is that in being virtuous we render a certain service to the gods, something the gods cannot do

---

[6] Taylor (1982), 112.

without us. It is not Taylor's view that, according to Socrates, the Greek word that means 'piety' (*to hosion* or *hē hosiotēs*) is synonymous with the word that means 'virtue' (*hē aretē*). It is rather that the capacity for being virtuous is identical with the capacity for being pious. Being virtuous is called being 'pious' when it is regarded under its theological aspect.[7]

I have no reason to deny that Socrates may have held such a view as the one Taylor suggests, or even that Plato might be somehow hinting in the *Euthyphro* that he did. But I am concerned that readers of this dialogue may become so preoccupied with figuring out what Socrates' views on piety 'really are', despite the protestations of Socratic ignorance, that they may miss the main point of the dialogue.

Socrates makes clear in the central argument of the dialogue (10a–11b) that he will not be satisfied until he is told what 'the pious' and 'the impious' *mean*. I say his quest for what piety is, is a search for meaning because the suggestion that the pious might be the god-loved is defeated by an argument that depends upon substituting 'god-loved' in a certain statement for 'pious'. That move can be defended only if what is under discussion is whether 'pious' means the same thing as 'god-loved'.

Although Taylor tells us it is Socrates' view that the capacity for being pious is identical with the capacity for being virtuous more generally, he allows that Socrates will not consider the relevant Greek terms synonymous. So what, in Socrates' view, does 'pious' mean? It means, Taylor says, *aretē pros ton theon* ('virtue toward, or with respect to, god'), where that gets glossed as meaning 'goodness of soul seen as man's contribution to the divine order of the universe'.[8] But that suggestion re-raises the main issue of the dialogue. What makes being virtuous a contribution to *God*'s order? Is it that virtue among human beings is the order God *wants* in the human part of the universe, that this is what is pleasing to God, or the gods? If so, we are back to the discredited suggestion, as indeed Socrates points out at the end of the dialogue. 'You surely remember that earlier the pious and the god-loved were shown not to be the same,

---

[7] This view is rather like Terry Penner's understanding of the unity of the virtues, which was mentioned in Ch. 3.

[8] Taylor (1982), 113.

but different from each other,' Socrates says there; 'or do you not remember?' (15c).

If, however, this contribution or service (*therapeia*) we make to God's order is something else besides the god-loved, what is it? Euthyphro in the dialogue is not able to make a satisfactory suggestion. And Socrates says his own hopes for learning what piety is are dashed by Euthyphro's refusal to continue the discussion. 'You have cast me down from a great hope I had,' he tells Euthyphro, in the last speech of the dialogue, 'that I would learn from you the nature of the pious and the impious' (15e).

The conclusion of the dialogue is thus that there is a problem, a puzzle, a perplexity, here.[9] Nothing that we might consider hinted at in the dialogue should blind us to the seriousness of the problem Socrates has confronted us with.

The Euthyphro Problem is indeed genuinely perplexing. It seems that the notion of piety includes essential reference to the attitude of God, or the gods. And yet, for that attitude to be appropriately divine, it seems that it, in turn, must appeal to a standard that should be normative for us human beings independently of its divine sanction. So there is a bind. It is not just unreflective religious believers who insist that morality must have its basis in divine approbation— as the enormous literature on 'Divine-Command Ethics', from ancient times down to the present, attests. Yet it remains difficult to see how divine sanction can be essential to normativity without that normativity losing its basis in reason.

Nor is the reach of the Euthyphro Problem restricted to God and ethics. It extends to any situation in which there is said to be a 'normative authority', in the sense that

(*a*) the judgement or ruling or preference of that authority seems to govern normative assessments in some domain, and also

(*b*) the authority figure is taken to have sufficient reason for making the judgements or rulings or expressing the preferences that are the relevant normative assessments.

---

[9] Many readers and commentators have been unwilling to accept the aporetic conclusion at face value. Among the recent ingenious efforts to find in the dialogue a positive account of what piety is, McPherran (1985) and (1995), as well as Calef (1995*a*) and (1995*b*), should be mentioned.

This means that everything from Supreme Court rulings to umpires' calls in baseball games raise the Euthyphro Problem.

In fact, I think the case of a baseball umpire's call is easier to handle than a ruling by the Supreme Court. Suppose the baseball umpire calls a given pitch a strike. We assume he made that call because, in his judgement, the baseball passed over the home plate within the box of space specified by the baseball rule book. But suppose that, as the instant replay on TV makes clear, the pitch did not really cross the plate within the prescribed space after all. And suppose that the umpire sticks by his call. What do we say? We can say that it was a strike because it was called a strike by the umpire. But we can add that it was not really a strike because it failed to cross the plate within the appropriate box. It was a strike and it wasn't a strike. But we can deal with the apparent contradiction by treating it as an equivocation.

What we do, in cases like this, is to make a distinction between what is determinative for a given game and what is definitive of the nature of a strike. When we say that it was a strike because the umpire called it one, we can interpret ourselves as meaning that it was determined to be a strike by the umpire, who mistakenly thought it had the nature of a strike as specified in the rule book.

I say the case of the Supreme Court is not so easy for several reasons. For one thing, the issues are typically not so clear-cut as baseball calls are. One reason they are not so clear-cut, is that questions about how to interpret the constitution, or the law, may be at issue, and not simply questions about how to apply a law whose meaning can be assumed to be clear. As part of the process of interpretation the Supreme Court is obliged to look at previous decisions, by previous Supreme Courts, as well as at decisions by lower courts. But the biggest difference is that in making its determinations the Supreme Court may be helping to define the key evaluative terms. So one can draw no simple contrast, as in baseball, between determining what a term or statute means and determining whether the term or statute has been applied correctly in the case under consideration.

In a way it can be quite correct to say that 'unconstitutional' means 'has been ruled unconstitutional by the Supreme Court'. Yet the court, in its opinions, gives reasons for its rulings, reasons that are by no means restricted to reciting previous rulings of the Supreme

Court. So when the court rules a given statute unconstitutional it does not usually mean by 'unconstitutional'—'has [already] been ruled unconstitutional by the Supreme Court'. The notion of unconstitutionality, as something partially, but not fully, determined by previous Supreme Court rulings, is, it seems, ineluctably problematic in a philosophical way that the Euthyphro Problem helps to bring out.

Whatever we end up saying about divine-approval ethics, or about unconstitutionality, or even about strikes in baseball, it seems clear that the Euthyphro Problem can easily astonish us with the surprise recognition that there is a basic puzzle we don't know how to deal with. In this astonished recognition there is a beginning for philosophy, as the figure of Socrates in Plato's *Euthyphro* shows us.

5

Shared Perplexity:
The Self-Stinging Stingray

PLATO'S dialogue *Meno* opens with a question from Meno about whether virtue can be taught. Socrates replies that, far from knowing whether or not virtue can be taught, he doesn't even know what virtue is (71a). There follows this characteristic avowal of what is called 'Socratic ignorance':

I myself, Meno, am as poor as my fellow citizens in this matter and I blame myself for my complete ignorance about virtue. If I do not know what something is, how could I know what qualities it possesses? (71b, Grube trans.)

Meno responds with disbelief. 'Do you really not know what virtue is? Are we to report this to the folk back home about you?'

Meno's questions are an effort to shame Socrates into admitting that he does, after all, know what virtue is. But Socrates refuses to be shamed. He goes on insisting that he does not know. He adds, 'I have never yet met anyone else who did know' (71c).

A reader may be forgiven for being sceptical about this claim of Socratic ignorance. If not quite insincere, it must surely be a serious overstatement. It cannot be that Socrates has 'complete ignorance about virtue' (*ouk eidōs peri aretēs to parapan*). Any intelligent speaker of the Greek language, having the ability to use correctly the Greek word for 'virtue', must have some idea what virtue is. Moreover, if Socrates really had complete ignorance about virtue, he could not, it seems, even ask intelligent questions about it, or tell whether answers to his questions were relevant to what was being asked about or directed to some quite different subject. (This last point invites a discussion of the Paradox of Inquiry, which is the subject of the next chapter.)

There are several things to say about such professions of Socratic ignorance. For one thing, Socrates isn't claiming any special, or unusual, gap in his knowledge. As he says here, he has never met any-one who *does* know what virtue is. So he thinks of the ignorance he is professing as a widely shared ignorance, perhaps even as a univer-sal ignorance.

Second, since the ignorance Socrates professes is quite compatible with his being able to ask astute and revealing questions about virtue, or whatever the matter under discussion is, it has to be a very special kind of ignorance. The picture we get from Plato's aporetic dialogues is that Socrates knows at least as much about the matter under discussion as his discussion partners know; but he, unlike them, realizes that there is some profound difficulty in what they otherwise naturally take themselves to understand perfectly well. His interlocutors have been unaware of this difficulty, but as they become aware of it, they begin to lose confidence that they can even use the ordinary words they had earlier used to express their easy-going intimations of knowledge. This is the phenomenon of having one's own words slip and slide around until one isn't sure any more what one is saying—precisely the phenomenon Euthyphro speaks of in the dialogue named after him, as we discussed in the last chapter.

A third thing to say is that Socrates' professions of ignorance gives us an important example of Socratic irony. Socrates, as Plato pre-sents him in the dialogues, is a sly old bird. He is often made to say things that strike a normal reader as disingenuous. When he says in the *Euthyphro*, as we noted in the last chapter, 'Then, Euthyphro, you must know what piety is', we naturally see him as insincerely set-ting up Euthyphro for a great fall. And when here in the *Meno* he blames himself for his 'complete ignorance about virtue', we natur-ally suspect him of a false, perhaps even an aggressive, humility. Is then the expression 'Socratic irony' just a polite and excessively deferential term for such objectionable disingenuousness? (It can cer-tainly turn off undergraduates who are being first introduced to Plato, as teachers of ancient philosophy have long come to realize.)

Even those of us who consider Socrates a philosophical hero, per-haps *the* philosophical hero, must admit that candour is not his long suit. As Plato presents him, he often seems wily, even scheming. I am convinced, however, that his disclaimers of knowledge have a deeply philosophical purpose. We are meant to realize, it seems, that matters we *all* assume we understand perfectly well may be philosophically problematic. Socrates' professions of ignorance are apparently meant to warn us of this important fact.

Gregory Vlastos, in his doggedly regimentational way, sees Socrates as equivocating on the Greek words for 'know', when he disavows having any knowledge of what, for example, virtue is. Vlastos finds in the Platonic corpus a difference between claims of knowledge, in a strong sense of 'know', and claims of knowledge in a weaker sense.[1] In the strong, 'certainty', sense, which Vlastos marks with a subscript 'c', everything I know is something I can be certain of; in the weaker, 'elenctic' sense, which Vlastos marks with a subscript 'e', what I know is only what is justifiable through elenctic cross-examination—the sort of questioning Socrates engages in, in the early Platonic dialogues.

I don't myself see that Socrates in Plato's early dialogues gives any evidence that he thinks of himself as equivocating on words for 'know' or 'knowledge'. But what I object to in the Vlastos reconstruction is not that it attributes to Socrates an alien metalinguistic distinction. My objection is that it distorts the Socratic purpose in disclaiming knowledge. As I read these dialogues, Socrates means to be saying something outrageous when he says he doesn't know at all what virtue is and has never met anyone who did. He means to shock us out of our complacent stupor. He realizes there is perplexity ahead that we hadn't suspected. He is warning us and also, of course, arousing our interest. If we read him as saying, in the pedantically circumspect fashion of Vlastos, 'Although I don't know with certainty what virtue is, I am able to put forward propositions about virtue that are elenctically justifiable', we will think we can safely sink back into our complacent stupor. ('So, what else is new?') By contrast, the perplexity Socrates means to arouse in Meno will lead Meno to say that he is not even sure he can use ordinary language about virtue anymore. What is more, Socrates will say that he shares fully in Meno's perplexity!

---

[1] 'Socrates' disavowal of knowledge', in Vlastos (1994), 39–66.

When Socrates tells Meno that he has never yet met anyone who knows what virtue is, he throws down the philosophical gauntlet. The two of them are off on a search for a definitional analysis of virtue. And the dialogue proceeds in a fashion characteristic of the early, definitional dialogues, such as *Laches* and *Euthyphro*.

The Greek word we translate as 'virtue' in these dialogues is *aretē*. It means 'excellence'. What Socrates is looking for in the *Meno*, one could say, is the nature of human excellence.

In the dialogue *Laches*, as we saw in Chapter 3, Socrates says it would be simply too daunting to begin with an investigation of 'the whole of virtue' (*peri holēs aretēs*) and suggests concentrating instead on only one part of virtue, namely, courage (190d). Later on in that same dialogue Socrates returns to the idea of virtue's parts. He mentions specifically temperance and justice as being, along with courage, parts of virtue (198a).

As we saw in Chapter 3, Socrates and his friends in the *Laches* land in perplexity because Socrates comes up with reasons for saying both that courage is only a part of virtue and also for saying that it is the whole of virtue (199e). That result seems to present them with a straightforward contradiction.

In the dialogue *Protagoras*, which is also thought to be an early dialogue, Plato has Socrates return to the idea that justice, temperance, and piety stand to virtue as parts to the whole. Socrates there asks Protagoras whether the individual virtues are parts of virtue in the way that the mouth, the nose, the eyes, and the ears are parts of a face? Or, he asks, are they rather parts in the way that sections of a bar of gold are parts of the whole bar (329d)? Protagoras opts for the face analogy. He insists that each part of virtue is not only different from the whole, but also different from each of the other parts.

In the *Meno* Socrates returns yet again to issues concerning virtue and the virtues, or, as he likes to put it, between the whole of virtue and its parts. Implicitly rejecting the suggestion of the *Laches* that it would be too daunting to investigate the whole of virtue, Socrates here sets out to do just that, or at least to get Meno to do it for him. Meno immediately divides virtue up into different parts. He speaks about the virtue of a man, the virtue of a woman, the virtue of a child, as well as the virtue of the elderly, and that of a free man or a slave.

There is no perplexity (*aporia*) about what virtue is, Meno says confidently, 'there is a virtue for every action and every age, for every task of ours and every one of us'. He adds, 'And Socrates, the same is true for wickedness' (72a).

In a move characteristic of Plato, Socrates responds to this proliferation of parts of virtue by saying that he wants Meno to tell him what all the parts of virtue have in common, 'the one and the same form (*eidos*) that makes them [all] virtues' (72c). Responding to Socrates' request for the common form that each 'part' of virtue shares with all the others, Meno tries out the suggestion that virtue is the ability to rule over people (73d). When Socrates gets Meno to concede that such ruling over others will not be virtuous unless it is just, he has an opportunity to point out that justice is one, and only one, of the individual virtues. Meno readily agrees and names courage, temperance, wisdom, and munificence as other virtues.

Socrates again complains that, whereas they were seeking the one thing that is virtue, what Meno has come up with is a whole laundry list of distinct virtues. 'Stop making many out of one, as jesters say whenever someone breaks something,' Socrates moans, 'but allow virtue to remain whole and sound and tell me what it is' (77ab).

In this set of exchanges Socrates faces us with a new question about the unity of the virtues. The question this time is not, as it was in the *Laches*, whether a person can be courageous without being wise. Nor is it the closely related question as to whether one can say what courage is without bringing in the demands that the other virtues lay on us. The problem now is to say what makes something count as *a* virtue. What do courage and justice and wisdom and piety and temperance all have in common that makes each of them a virtue?

One might try saying that what all these individual virtues have in common is simply that they belong to the list of things that are virtues. In effect, Meno tries out that move. But Socrates will not accept it. Each of these individual virtues must, he insists, have some form or character in common with all the rest, something that makes them each and all of them virtues. He wants to know what that common form is.

Is Socrates here making appeal to the Platonic Theory of Forms? Not necessarily. He can be thinking of the common form (*eidos*), or characteristic (*idea*), as a feature specifiable by definition without supposing, as the Theory of Forms would have it, that this form or characteristic is an eternal and unchanging substance.

In any case, Socrates' question is a deep one, and a deeply problematic one. We might try answering by saying that moral virtues are those traits of character such that each one, by itself, tends to make one morally better than one would be without it. But, in the light of what Socrates says in the *Laches*, this will not be satisfactory. It assumes that we could take the character traits, one at a time, and ask how morally good a person would be with or without just that particular trait. But part of the implication of the doctrine of the unity of the virtues is that we can't do that. Since we can't separate courage cleanly from, say, wisdom, we can't really ask what moral worth courage, just by itself, adds to a courageous person, or detracts from a non-courageous one.

If we look ahead in Plato's writings, we can see that, in the *Republic*, Plato helps himself to an account of what makes temperance, courage, wisdom, and justice count as virtues by arguing for a tripartite division of the soul. Courage is the peculiar virtue of the spirited part, wisdom is the peculiar virtue of the rational part. Temperance is said to be an agreement between the parts, where the rational part is said to be the ruler that keeps the spirited and appetitive parts under rational control. And justice consists in each part doing its own work, the tasks peculiar to it. On the basis of this account one could say that for someone to have an individual virtue is for the relevant part of that person's soul to perform its function well (that goes for courage and wisdom) or else for the parts to be harmonious (temperance) and each doing 'its own thing' (justice).

Although the account of what a virtue is that is to be found in the *Republic* is certainly very attractive, it has obvious limitations. For one thing, it leaves out virtues that Plato himself recognizes in other works, such as piety and munificence (*Meno* 74a). Could one expand the *Republic* approach to accommodate them?

The natural thing to do to try to make the *Republic* scheme work for other virtues would be to find other parts of the soul besides the appetite, the spirited part, and the rational part. A natural candidate for this kind of analysis might be piety. It is often said that human beings have an innate religious sense. One might try arguing that there is a religious part of the soul, such that when that part functions well, the person whose soul it is, is pious.

Even if we could accommodate piety in this way, it is less tempting to suppose that there is a part of the soul whose special excellence is munificence, or that munificence might be some special relationship between the parts of the soul. And what about other virtues? Aristotle seems willing to consider honesty, or truthfulness (*alētheia*), a virtue (*Nicomachean Ethics* 4. 7). It seems quite inappropriate to look for a part of the soul whose excellence of function might be truthfulness.

Aristotle, by appeal to his Doctrine of the Mean, does gives us this definition of a virtue:

Virtue, then, is a state of character concerned with choice, lying in a mean, i.e. the mean relative to us, this being determined by a rational principle, and by that principle by which the man of practical wisdom would determine it. (*Nicomachean Ethics* 2. 6, 1106^{b}36, Ross trans.)

One has to add, in candour, that it has not been entirely clear to commentators exactly how Aristotle's definition is supposed to work, or whether it manages to pick out all and only those states of character that Aristotle considers virtues. But certainly Plato's Socrates never comes close to offering any such definition; nor do his interlocutors.

Meno's best effort in the dialogue named after him to say what virtue is, as a whole, comes at 77b. It is that virtue is 'to desire beautiful, or noble, things (*tōn kalōn*) and have the power to acquire them'. 'Good' is soon substituted for 'beautiful' (or 'noble') and so (*a*) desiring good things and (*b*) having the power to get them becomes the suggested analysis.

This definitional analysis is rejected in two stages. In the first stage, Socrates argues that clause (*a*) is vacuous, since everybody desires good things and nobody wants bad ones. The idea that nobody wants bad things is identified in the literature as a Socratic paradox and this part of the refutation has garnered much commentary and discussion.

Without wishing in any way to minimize the interest and importance of Socrates' reasoning for the conclusion that no one wants bad things, I wish to turn to the refutation of clause (*b*). The reason I wish to concentrate on it is that it concerns the relation between virtue and the virtues.

In arguing that clause (*a*) is vacuous, Socrates leaves Meno with the suggestion that virtue is simply the power to acquire good things (78bc). Socrates suggests that those good things might include health and wealth, and Meno adds to the list of goods: gold, silver, honour, and offices in the city. Socrates then asks whether it matters how these good things are acquired, whether, say, justly and piously—or whether it does not matter how we get them. He wins assent to his assertion that 'the acquisition must be accompanied by justice or moderation or piety or some other part of virtue' (78e).

Socrates then protests that, once we add the needed qualification, we will have attempted to define the whole of virtue by reference to one, or perhaps more than one, of its parts. He protests:

When I begged you to tell me about virtue as a whole, you are far from telling me what it is. Rather, you say that every action is virtue if it is performed with a part of virtue, as if you had told me what virtue as a whole is, and I would already know that, even if you fragment it into parts.   (79bc, Grube trans.)

Socrates' idea seems to be that virtue as a whole is the genus, virtue, and the individual virtues, such as justice, piety, and temperance, are parts of that whole in the sense of being species, or kinds, of virtue. He then seems to be making the natural assumption that to provide a definitional analysis of one part or species of virtue, say, justice, we would need to say what kind or species of virtue it is. But if our definitional analysis of virtue as a whole, that is, the genus, virtue, included a reference to one species, say, justice, then the analysis would be circular. Thus to say that virtue is having the power to acquire good things *justly*, where 'justly' is 'in accordance with such-and-such a kind of virtue', would be to say that virtue is having the power to acquire good things in accordance with such-and-such virtue. And clearly that won't do. As Socrates tells Meno, 'You must not think that, while the nature of virtue as a whole [i.e. as genus] is still under inquiry, you can make its nature clear by answering in terms of the parts [kinds or species] of virtue' (79d).

The objection is one of circularity. But it is also deeper than even that. Suppose we add 'justly' to 'having the power to acquire good things'. Then either acquiring good things justly necessarily includes acquiring them according to all the other virtues, or it doesn't. If it does include all the others, because of the unity of the virtues, then adding 'justly' is, in effect, adding 'virtuously'. If it doesn't, then we need to make sure that each of the other virtues is specified in the definition as well. We will need to know what all the other virtues are, if we are to eliminate the possibility that, say, acquiring good things impiously, or intemperately, or whatever, counts as an exercise of virtue. But we will not be able to use our definitional analysis of virtue to determine which character traits count as virtues; indeed we will need to use our list of character traits that count as virtues to say what virtue is! We will have failed completely to say what the common form is, that makes all the individual virtues count as virtues. Here we need to recall Socrates' earlier protest:

Even if [the virtues] are many and various, all of them have one and the same form (*eidos*) which makes them virtues, and it is right to look to this when one is asked to make clear what virtue is. (72b, Grube trans.)

At this point in the proceedings Socrates tells Meno they must start over and try again to say what virtue is (79e). Meno responds with one of the most famous speeches in the Platonic corpus. We may want to consider it the central text for our whole discussion of Socratic perplexity:

Socrates, before I even met you I used to hear that you are always being perplexed (*aporeis*) and that you make others perplexed (*aporein*), and now I think you are bewitching and beguiling me, simply putting me under a spell, so that I am full of perplexity (*aporias*) . . . you seem . . . to be like the broad torpedo fish, for it too makes anyone who comes close and touches it feel numb, you seem to have that kind of effect on me, for both my mind and my tongue are numb, and I have no answer to give you. Yet I have made many speeches about virtue before large audiences on a thousand occasions, very good speeches as I thought, but now I cannot say what [virtue] is. (*Meno* 79e–80b, Grube trans., modified)

This speech gives us, one could say, the canonical expression of Socratic perplexity. Yet the picture is not complete without Socrates' response. 'Now if the torpedo fish is itself numb, and so makes others numb', Socrates says,

then I resemble it, but not otherwise, for I am not myself free of perplexity (*euporōn*) when I make others perplexed (*aporein*); but I am more perplexed (*aporōn*) than anyone when I make others perplexed (*aporein*).   (80cd)

Looking back to Socrates' claim of ignorance at 71b we can see now that Socrates thinks he doesn't know at all what virtue is because he doesn't know how to resolve basic problems about how to define 'virtue'. He doesn't know how to offer a satisfactory definition of 'virtue as a whole'; and he doesn't know how to define 'virtue' in such a way as to make clear why temperance, courage, wisdom, justice, piety, and munificence count as individual virtues. Yet he knows as well as other intelligent Greek speakers how to use the Greek word for virtue. And he appreciates in a way that few others could improve on the problematic nature of any serious attempt to say what virtue and the virtues are.

6

Avoiding Perplexity:
The Paradox of Inquiry

THE picture of Socrates as a self-stinging stingray is a profoundly memorable one. Many of us were first won over to philosophy by a teacher who could pace back and forth in front of a class and wrestle publicly, and inconclusively, with endlessly engrossing questions about free will and determinism, or the problem of other minds, or the nature of causality. In other subjects, a teacher might be expected to know the answer to almost all questions students are capable of even formulating. Not so in philosophy. Here the most memorable teachers may be just as adept at getting themselves perplexed, as they are at inducing perplexity in the philosophical neophytes they teach. Strange subject!

Where will it lead? Will it *lead* anywhere? Fully managed perplexity induced by an unperplexed teacher is one thing. But perplexity that numbs the teacher as much as it paralyses the pupils threatens inconclusiveness, indirection, and failure. Again, it is Meno who makes this threat of indirection and inconclusiveness clear. Thus, just after Socrates insists in the *Meno* that he shares in the perplexity he induces in others, he admits, yet again, that he himself does not know what virtue is; he invites Meno to join with him in a fresh effort to find out what it is. Meno, however, has become suspicious of the whole enterprise. 'How will you look for it, Socrates,' he asks,

when you do not know at all what it is? How will you aim to search for something you do not know at all? If you should meet with it, how will you know that this is the thing that you did not know? (80d)

Socrates responds:

I know what you want to say, Meno. Do you realize what a debater's argument [or: contentious argument, *eristikon logon*] you are bringing up, that a man cannot search either for what he knows or for what he does not know. He cannot search for what he knows—since he knows it, there is no need to search—nor for what he does not know, for he does not know what to look for.   (80de, Grube trans.)

Socrates recognizes in Meno's question what has come to be called 'the Paradox of Inquiry'. According to this paradox, we cannot seek to find out what we already know; in that case, there is nothing for us to find out. On the other hand, where, as in the inquiry about what virtue is, the object of the inquiry and the nature of that object are one and the same thing,[1] we cannot aim our inquiry at its object, or recognize it when it turns up, unless we already know what it is, that is, know how to distinguish it from things easily confused with it. Assuming, as Socrates apparently does here, that either one already knows what virtue is or one simply doesn't know what it is—that is, assuming there is no intermediate state between knowing and simply not knowing—then there can be no inquiry into what virtue is.

I myself find the Paradox of Inquiry very perplexing. Surprisingly, Socrates, in the dialogue, seems not to. Although he and Meno have just expressed a deep, and at least in Meno's case, paralysing perplexity about what virtue is, Socrates seems not to consider the Paradox of Inquiry comparably perplexing or paralysing. Why not?

Perhaps the way Socrates characterizes this paradox is meant to give us one clue as to why he is not perplexed by it. He calls it an *eristikos logos*, an 'eristic' or contentious argument. He thus links it with a stylized form of debate developed by the sophists and called 'eristic'. Since Plato devotes his dialogue *Euthydemus* to sophistic eristic, one might hope to find in that dialogue some clue as to what Plato means by having Socrates call the Paradox of Inquiry an eristic argument, and also some clue as to why Socrates, in the *Meno*, should fail to find the paradox perplexing.[2]

---

[1] Nicholas White puts the point this way: 'Plato does think of the effort to "know" an object as a kind of search for it . . . [He also thinks] of it as an effort to say "what the object is", i.e., to produce a certain sort of definition or specification of it . . .' (White (1974), 291).

[2] Nicholas White protests: 'A mistranslation of "*eristikon*" at 80e2 has helped to foster the idea that Plato does not take the paradox seriously. There is no reason to render the word here by "sophistical"; it means simply "contentious" or "obstructionist" . . .' (White (1974), 289 n, 1). My point, however, is that Plato does not have

The first two eristic arguments in the *Euthydemus* do indeed bear some significant resemblance to the Paradox of Inquiry; the second of these, in particular, is often linked with it by commentators. In what follows I shall focus on it. In that argument, the sophist, Euthydemus, asks the boy, Kleinias, the question, 'Do learners learn [or: understand, *manthanō*] things they know or things they do not know?' (*Euthydemus* 276d). Kleinias, who had expressed perplexity about how to deal with the first eristic question put to him (275d), plunges right in this time. He answers, sensibly enough, that learners learn things they do not know (276e).

To understand how the discussion goes on from here, we need to realize, what Socrates later points out (at 277ab), that the governing verb in Euthydemus' question, *manthanō*, may indeed mean 'learn', but it may also mean 'understand'. To mimic the Greek I shall make up the verb, 'manthanize', and stipulate that it, like its Greek proto-type, may also mean either 'learn' or 'understand'. In a context in which it means 'learn' I shall write 'manthanize (learn)'. In a context in which it means 'understand' I shall write 'manthanize (under-stand)'. Where its meaning is indeterminate between these two possibilities, I shall write 'manthanize' either without parenthetical specification, or with the disjunctive specification, '(learn/under-stand)'. Reformulated according to this procedure, Euthydemus' question is whether learners manthanize (learn/understand) what they know or what they do not know.

Euthydemus now imagines a teacher dictating the answer to be manthanized (learned) and points out that, to be able to take the dic-tation, that is, to be able to write down what is being dictated, the learner would have to know the alphabet. Euthydemus then insists that, in already knowing all the letters in which the answer will be stated, the learner already manthanizes (understands) what is being dictated to him. Thus in the imagined case, the learner manthanizes (understands) what he knows. So Kleinias' answer (that learners manthanize things they don't know) is wrong.

Socrates in the dialogue express *aporia* about it. Meno is allowed to express puzzle-ment over it, but Socrates isn't. I agree with White, however, that Plato has Socrates develop a rather grand response to it, even though he resists being puzzled by it.

When Euthydemus' luckless interlocutor tries accepting the other horn of the dilemma (that learners manthanize things they already know), Euthydemus replies, scornfully, that learning is acquiring knowledge one did not have before. Thus it can't be the case that learners manthanize (learn) things they already know (277c). With both horns of the dilemma rejected, we are to conclude that learners don't manthanize (learn/understand) anything.

It is surely arguments like this that make us think sophists deserve their bad name. Socrates, in the dialogue, seems to agree; he suggests that such arguments serve no serious purpose. He characterizes these eristic arguments in the following way:

> These things are the frivolous part of study (which is why I also tell you that the men are jesting); and I call these things 'frivolity' because even if a man were to learn many or even all such things, he would be none the wiser as to how matters stand but would only be able to make fun of people, tripping them up and overturning them by means of the distinctions in words, just like the people who pull the chair out from under a man who is going to sit down and then laugh gleefully when they see him sprawling on his back. (278b, Sprague trans.)

If the Paradox of Inquiry really does resemble this eristic argument from the dialogue *Euthydemus*, it is quite reasonable that Socrates in the *Meno* should refuse to be perplexed by it. But is the resemblance more than superficial? Is bringing up the Paradox of Inquiry really like pulling the chair out from under people at a party and then laughing gleefully as one sees the victims 'sprawling on their backs'?

To answer those questions, let us now restate the premises that make up the two arguments. In comparing the second eristic argument from the *Euthydemus* with the Paradox of Inquiry I am going to make superficial adjustments in the formulation of the *Euthydemus* argument to make clearer its similarity to the Paradox of Inquiry. Thus instead of asking whether 'learners learn', I shall say, 'If you can learn something', etc. Transformed in this fashion, here is the way the second eristic argument from the *Euthydemus* begins:

    (1) If you can manthanize (learn/understand) something, then either

    (*a*) what you manthanize (*understand*) is something you don't
        (already) know; or else
    (*b*) what you manthanize (*learn*) is something you do
        (already) know.[3]

Both (*a*) and (*b*) are rejected. We are thus to conclude, by *modus tollens*:

    (2) You can't manthanize (learn/understand) anything.

The argument is clearly fallacious. What gives (1), without the parenthetical specification of senses, its initial plausibility is the appearance that its disjunctive consequent covers all the logical possibilities. But when we become clear that 'manthanize' needs to be disambiguated, these four possibilities present themselves:

    (i) What you understand is something you don't (already) know.
    (ii) What you understand is something you do (already) know.
    (iii) What you learn is something you don't (already) know.
    (iv) What you learn is something you do (already) know.

The disjunctive consequent of (1) actually covers, given the way Euthydemus interprets it, only two of these four possibilities, namely (i) and (iv). Once we understand that, (1) loses all plausibility.

The Paradox of Inquiry can be laid out in a similar way, but without any need for equivocation in the statement of it. In analogy to (1) above, we begin with this:

    (3) If you can search (successfully) for something, then either
    (*a*) what you (successfully) search for is something you don't
        (already) know; or else
    (*b*) what you (successfully) search for is something you do
        (already) know.[4]

---

[3] This reconstruction is inspired by remarks Charles Kahn made to me in reviewing an earlier draft of this chapter. I am not sure whether he would like the way I have put his remarks to use.

[4] This, again, is a departure from Plato's syntax. G. M. A. Grube translates, '. . . a man cannot search either for what he knows or for what he does not know?' (80e). 'The thing which he knows' would be syntactically closer to Plato, but it is so artificial in English that it numbs our philosophical intuitions. It seems to me that (3) captures the puzzle better.

Meno offers reasons for rejecting both (*a*) and (*b*). We are thus led, again by *modus tollens*, to reject the antecedent and conclude that there is no such thing as a successful search for anything.

Meno offers two different reasons for rejecting alternative (*a*). The first reason is that, if you don't already know, for example, what virtue is, you won't be able to aim your search properly at the target, that is, aim it at virtue (80d). The idea is that a search that is not targeted specifically at virtue, as distinct from all the things similar to it and easily confused with it, is not really a search specifically for virtue and therefore cannot be called a successful search for virtue. Let's call this 'the Targeting Objection' to the first horn of (3). It seems quite plausible.

Wouldn't it be possible, however, one might ask oneself, to have a search that was successful, not because it was targeted properly, but rather because the search just *happened* to hit its target? That brings us to Meno's second point. It is that those who don't already know what virtue is will not be able to recognize virtue, even if they stumble on it. Let's call this 'the Recognition Objection' to the first horn of (3). The idea is that a search conducted without the ability to recognize virtue, even if virtue should be eventually encountered, unrecognized, is not really a search specifically for virtue. The Recognition Objection, too, seems quite telling. Together these two objections seem to rule out the possibility of a successful search for virtue when one doesn't know what it is. Thus, the first horn of the dilemma is eliminated.

The second horn of the dilemma is much easier to eliminate. Suppose you do already know what virtue is. Ruling out the possibility that

(*b*) what you (successfully) search for is something you do (already) know

hardly needs much discussion. After all, a search for what you already have is not a genuine search at all. You can't search for something you already have.

Having ruled out both (*a*) and (*b*) of (3), we may thus conclude, by *modus tollens*,

(4) You can't search for anything [and, in particular, you can't search for what virtue is].

How similar is this argument to the eristic argument discussed above from the *Euthydemus*? It is quite similar in its second half. Thus, the reason offered for rejecting the second horn of the *Euthydemus* dilemma—that learning is acquiring knowledge one already has—is as good as the reason offered for rejecting the second horn of the Paradox of Inquiry—that searching for what you already know is no search at all. Moreover, these reasons are similar, as well as being similarly good.

The big difference between the two arguments is that the *Euthydemus* argument requires an equivocation on 'manthanize', whereas no equivocation at all is required to fall into the grip of the Paradox of Inquiry. The eristic argument from the *Euthydemus* is thus sophistical in the popular (pejorative) sense that it requires a wordplay to produce its paradoxical result. The Paradox of Inquiry, by contrast, depends on no wordplay. It can induce perplexity even when the meanings of the constituent terms are kept constant throughout.

Someone might well want to reject this last claim and insist that the plausibility of (3) does indeed rest on an equivocation. 'I know what I am searching for' might mean either 'I have an adequate *description* or *specification* under which I am searching for something' or 'I know the thing itself I am searching for.' Thus it is in the second sense that I know what I am searching for when I rifle the attic for my favourite sweater. But it is in the first sense that I look through town records to find the oldest house in town. I can certainly know what I am searching for by searching under the quite adequate description 'oldest house in town', even though I am quite unfamiliar with the actual building that turns out to satisfy that description.

Having offered these two interpretations of 'I know what I am searching for', the critic can then maintain that the best response to the Paradox of Inquiry is to grasp the second horn of the dilemma and interpret 'you know what you are searching for' to mean 'you have an adequate description or specification of what you are searching for'. So understood, this horn leaves open the possibility that one hasn't yet found the object that fits the description under which one is searching; thus the search can be perfectly genuine.

I concede that this diagnosis of equivocation is an excellent response to the Paradox of Inquiry conceived in its most general form. When, however, the search envisaged is clearly a philosophical one, for example, a search for what virtue is, then part of the inquiry may well be an investigation into whether we really have any adequate description or specification of what virtue is. (See n. 1.)

A persistent critic may not want to accept that response. 'Surely,' this critic may insist, 'there is *some* description of what virtue is under which you can be said to conduct your search, even if it is only this: "what most people call 'virtue' ".' But Socrates would not, I think, accept that way out. If he were primarily interested in finding out what most people call 'virtue', he could be doing empirical linguistics, but he wouldn't be doing philosophy. Since his inquiry is a genuinely philosophical one, it is open to him to conclude, as a result of his inquiry, that virtue is really something quite different from what most people call 'virtue'. So we can't be sure that even such a minimal specification as 'what most people call "virtue" ' will be adequate to search under. We cannot, therefore, safely grasp the second horn of the dilemma and say that we know what we are searching for in the sense of having at least an adequate description or specification of what virtue is.

A second critic may try a different tack. Socrates himself does go on in the dialogue to recognize, this critic may point out, two different senses of 'know'. The distinction he draws, my critic may say, is a central implication of the Theory of Recollection (*anamnēsis*), which Socrates introduces this way:

As the soul is immortal, has been born often and has seen all things here and in the underworld, there is nothing which it has not learned; so it is in no way surprising that it can recollect the things it knew before, both about virtue and other things. As the whole of nature is akin, and the soul has learned everything, nothing prevents a man, after recalling one thing only—a process men call learning—discovering everything else for himself, if he is brave and does not tire of the search, for searching and learning are, as a whole, recollection. We must, therefore, not believe that debater's argument [eristic argument, *tō eristikō logō*], for it would make us idle, and faint-hearted men like to hear it, whereas my argument makes them energetic and keen on the search. I trust that this is true, and I want to inquire along with you into the nature of virtue.   (81c–e, Grube trans.)

I might try to respond to this second critic by insisting that Plato does not, in this passage anyway, explicitly distinguish senses of the verb for 'know'. But I want to be conciliatory on that point. I don't see that it really matters much whether we understand Socrates here to be distinguishing two ways of knowing (knowing 'before', in a previous existence, and knowing now), or to be marking off two senses of 'know'. Let's choose the second alternative so as to facilitate the comparison with the *Euthydemus* discussion, where a distinction between senses is explicitly drawn.[5]

First, there will be, according to Socrates, a purely latent sense of 'know'. What I can be said to know in this sense includes everything the soul 'brings with it' at birth, even things I have not as yet 'recalled'. Second, there is an active or manifest sense of 'know'. What I know in this sense includes all knowledge currently accessible to me. With this distinction in mind we can specify two different versions of (3), namely, (3L), which uses 'know' in the latent sense, and (3M), which uses 'know' in the manifest sense:

(3M) If you can search (successfully) for something, then either
    (*a*) what you (successfully) search for is something you don't (already) know, in the *manifest* sense of 'know'; or else
    (*b*) what you (successfully) search for is something you do (already) know, in the *manifest* sense of 'know'.

(3L) If you can search (successfully) for something, then either
    (*a*) what you (successfully) search for is something you don't (already) know, in the *latent* sense of 'know'; or else
    (*b*) what you (successfully) search for is something you do (already) know, in the *latent* sense of 'know'.

It is important to note that I have applied the manifest/latent distinction in such a way that the sense of 'know' does not shift *within* a given reading of (3). The result is that in each case the disjunctive

---

[5] Socrates, appealing to Prodicus, makes a distinction between two different senses of 'learn' to defuse the first eristic argument and then says, 'There was something similar to this in the second question, when they asked you whether people learn what they know or what they do not know' (277ab, Sprague trans.). Presumably the equivocation in this case is on 'know'.

consequent of (3)—the two horns of the dilemma—genuinely exhausts the possibilities. This preserves the plausibility of (3), whether read as (3M) or as (3L). Thus, unlike the fully explicated argument from the *Euthydemus*, the Paradox of Inquiry does not commit the fallacy of equivocation.

Socrates' solution is now to say that, whether we understand (3) as (3M) or as (3L), one horn of the dilemma can be accepted. In (3M) it is the first horn that can be accepted. Searching for what virtue is, is an effort to make manifest what is, so far, only latent knowledge. In (3L), by contrast, it is the second horn that is acceptable. You already know latently what you are searching for and trying to make manifest.

If I am right in thinking that this is Socrates' idea, then we are to suppose that, when we have only latent knowledge of what virtue is, there is 'room' left to add manifest knowledge. Moreover, having latent knowledge should be enough to enable us to recognize it, should we stumble on it. Perhaps, once I have 'encountered' and recognized virtue, I can then describe it, that is, define 'virtue', despite the fact that beforehand I would not have been able to say what I was looking for. That seems to be a situation we are often in with respect to people and places we haven't seen for a long time. If the analogy is appropriate, it should help us understand how we can successfully search for what virtue is. That answers the Recognition Objection.

The point about needing to aim the search, the Targeting Objection, is trickier to deal with. On this point, here is the crucial part of Socrates' solution:

As the whole of nature is akin, and the soul has learned everything, nothing prevents a man, after recalling one thing only—a process men call learning—discovering everything else for himself, if he is brave and does not tire of the search, for searching and learning are, as a whole, recollection. (81d, Grube trans.)

Is all this plausible? It seems plausible to suppose that virtue belongs to a network of other natures in such a way that, if one has indeed latched onto a single item in the network, one has a good chance to work out from there until the whole network can be recovered. Perhaps the hardest thing to accept is the idea that one might just happen on the first item and recognize it, *unerringly*, for the bit of real knowledge that it is. (There are lots of passages in Plato that suggest the recognition must be unerring, or infallible, if it is to count as yielding knowledge, for example, *Republic* 477e.)

In any case we can see in Socrates' response to the Paradox of Inquiry that he is willing to make two quite grand assumptions to underwrite the legitimacy of philosophical inquiry. One is that all nature is akin. The other is that we all have latent knowledge of what virtue is and that it is available for recollection. With the assumption of latent knowledge there is some hope that Socratic inquiry will trigger an 'aha! experience', an intuition of correctness based on latent, though previously merely latent, knowledge.

Are, then, Socratic inquiries limited to what, in a court of law, might be dismissed as mere 'fishing expeditions', that is, undirected explorations that might, or might not, terminate in, say, discovering what virtue is? Here is where the second assumption comes in. Socrates asks us to assume that the world of nature is interrelated in such a way that, once we have recovered one bit of latent knowledge, reflection on it will naturally lead to the recovery of other bits.

Looking ahead to the positive conclusions of Plato's *Republic*, we might imagine how this second assumption could work out in practice. Suppose one stumbled on the intuition that the individual virtue, wisdom, is simply the *ergon idion*, the proper work or functioning, of that part of the soul we call 'reason'. Having received a certifying 'aha! experience' with this intuition, we might naturally try to delineate another part of the soul and its proper functions. We might expect that there would be a specific virtue to go with the proper function of the 'spirited' part of the soul (courage). We might also expect that temperance would be the excellence of appetite but then, on reflection, decide that temperance is more general than that and conclude that it is a kind of harmony of the whole. And one might somehow be led to suppose that justice consists in each part of the soul doing its proper work. That is, of course, exactly what Socrates tells us about the virtues in book 4 of the *Republic*.

Is it reasonable to accept these two assumptions—that we have already known these things before and that all nature is akin? The only justification Socrates offers for them in the *Meno* is a pragmatic one. 'We must, therefore, not believe that *eristic* reasoning', he admonishes Meno,

for it would make us idle, [and] fainthearted . . . whereas this reasoning makes them energetic and keen on the search. Being convinced of its truth, I am ready with your help, to inquire into the nature of virtue.   (81de, Grube trans.)

A later passage is even more explicitly pragmatic. It almost sounds like William James:

I shouldn't like to take my oath on the whole story, but one thing I am ready to fight for as long as I can, in word and act—that is, that we shall be better, braver, and more active men if we believe it right to look for what we don't know than if we believe there is no point in looking because what we don't know we can never discover.   (86bc, Grube trans.)

Can we now say how Socrates defuses the perplexity that the Paradox of Inquiry threatens? I think we can. He defuses it by distinguishing 'know' in the sense of knowing latently and 'know' in the sense of knowing manifestly. But to make good on this solution he has to develop both the Theory of Recollection and the hypothesis that all nature is akin. As if expecting us to be a little sceptical about the Theory of Recollection and uncertain about the hypothesis that all nature is akin, Socrates also warns us not to be lulled into faint-hearted inactivity by the Paradox of Inquiry. We will be better and braver, he assures us, if we press on with the inquiry.

Can we now explain why Socrates disparages the Paradox of Inquiry by calling it an 'eristic argument'? As we have seen, his disparagement does not prevent him from responding to the argument with quite grand metaphysical assumptions. He clearly thinks the challenge it presents is worthy of such a serious response. In calling the reasoning 'eristic' he may only mean that (*a*) the Paradox of Inquiry is a dilemma and (*b*) thinking about it will lead us to distinguish two senses of a key word. If, however, that is indeed his point, then we should protest that we ought to distinguish

    (*a*) dilemmas that derive their power to perplex us from an unacknowledged and invalidating equivocation from

(*b*) dilemmas that have the power to perplex us without relying on an equivocation at all, even if, to defuse their power to perplex us, we need to make more specific the sense in which we understand some key term.

With respect to the Paradox of Inquiry Socrates can give Meno his choice as to which sense of 'know' he has in mind. Whichever sense Meno chooses, Socrates thinks he can grasp successfully one horn of the dilemma that Meno has offered him. Thus even if the Paradox of Inquiry is an eristic argument in the unobjectionable sense that it is a dilemma that will lead us to distinguish two senses of some key term to rob it of its force, it is not an eristic argument in the pejorative sense that it gains its power to puzzle and perplex us by shifting, fallaciously, from one sense of a key term to the other.

Socrates, in the *Meno*, seems determined to do what he can to keep both himself and his interlocutor from becoming benumbed by the Paradox of Inquiry. This effort to steer the investigation clear of perplexity, instead of inducing perplexity, as Socrates had done so masterfully in the first part of the dialogue, marks an important shift in Socrates' role in the *Meno*. The shift to this new role needs to be put together with another surprising development in the *Meno*, one that I shall be discussing in the next chapter.

7

Purely Instrumental Perplexity

To illustrate the thesis that seeking and learning are simply recollection Socrates, in the dialogue *Meno*, asks Meno to call one of his servants, or house-boys, for Socrates to interrogate him. Meno does as requested. Then Socrates, having first established that the slave-boy before him is a Greek and speaks the language, sets him a geometrical problem. Socrates wants the slave-boy to tell him how to construct a square with an area twice that of a given square.

In one of the most famous passages in the whole Platonic corpus, Socrates questions the slave-boy and gets him to reflect on his first mistaken answers until finally the boy is able to say, for himself, that the way to double the size of a given square is to construct a square on the diagonal of that square (*Meno* 85b). In the middle of the interrogation of the slave-boy, Socrates pauses for this exchange with Meno:

SOCRATES: Observe, Meno, the stage he has reached on the path of recollection. At the beginning he did not know the side of the square of eight feet. Nor indeed does he know it now, but then he thought he knew it and answered boldly, as was appropriate—he felt no perplexity (*aporein*). Now however he does feel perplexed (*aporein*). Not only does he not know the answer, he doesn't even think he knows.

MENO: Quite true.

SOCRATES: Isn't he in a better position now in relation to what he didn't know?

MENO: I admit that too.

SOCRATES: So in perplexing him (*aporein oun auton poiēsantes*) and numbing him like the stingray, have we done him any harm?

MENO: I think not.

SOCRATES: In fact we have helped him to some extent toward finding out the right answer, for now not only is he ignorant of it but he will be quite glad to look for it. Up to now, he thought he could speak well and fluently, on many occasions and before large audiences, on the subject of a square double the size of a given square, maintaining that it must have a side of double the length.

(84a–c, Guthrie trans.)

Several things about this passage are worth commenting on. First, although Socrates explicitly recalls the image of the stingray he has taken over from Meno, and although he explicitly claims to be perplexing and numbing the slave-boy like the stingray, he has apparently dropped the requirement that he will accept the analogy only if the stingray also stings itself. This is a very surprising development. It is surprising for several different reasons.

It is quite plausible to think of a seasoned philosopher like Socrates as remaining perplexed about what virtue is, even after having had many discussions with many people on this subject. So when, a few pages earlier in the dialogue, Socrates had insisted that he is just as perplexed about what virtue is as Meno, and when he adds that his questioning numbs himself just as much as it numbs Meno, we can accept that. This is the picture of what I called in Chapter 5 'shared perplexity'. In so far as this picture fits the philosopher as a general thing, the implication is that the philosopher inquires about matters so deeply problematic that even a seasoned questioner like Socrates may still find the matter under investigation utterly baffling.

All of us who teach philosophy have had the experience of being perplexed about the topic we are to lecture on, or discuss in a seminar. It belongs to our calling. Suppose I am asked to teach an introductory course in aesthetics, even though I have never taught aesthetics before and even though I have no worked-out views in the philosophy of art that I want to defend or transmit to others. The biggest constraint on my chances of success in carrying out this assignment will not be my ability to come up with a defensible theory of, for example, what makes something count as a work of art. The biggest constraint on my chances of success will be my ability to get myself perplexed about, say, whether Marcel Duchamp's famous urinal, which he called 'Fountain', is or is not a work of art, and why, or why not. If I can get myself perplexed about this question, I have a very good chance of getting my students perplexed and thereby motivating them to consider, with me, the various theories that have been offered in response to this sort of question. But if I cannot get myself perplexed about this question, I have very little chance of getting my students interested in theories about what makes something an art object.

When Socrates begins his questioning of the slave-boy, not about what virtue is, but about how to construct a square with an area twice that of a given square, he is turning from a deeply problematic question to a question which, though difficult, is not really problematic at all. In this case there is clearly a satisfactory answer to the question and anyone even moderately schooled in geometry ought to be able to discover what it is. It is worth noting that, whereas still being seriously perplexed about what makes Duchamp's urinal count, or fail to count, as a work of art speaks in favour of my candidacy to teach the course in aesthetics, being still puzzled about how to construct a square with an area twice that of a given square should disqualify me as a candidate for teaching a course in geometry. That fact tells us something very important about both philosophy and geometry.

Of course, a geometry teacher may want to make a geometry pupil perplexed, even perplexed about 'the square of double size'. Indeed, inducing perplexity may be the most effective way to prod the geometry pupil into the hard reflection required to come by the right answer, or to appreciate and understand the correctness of an answer once it has been arrived at. Still, such perplexity will have only the instrumental value of stimulating the learner to think hard enough to arrive at, and understand, the correct answer. Once the answer has been found, and understood, there is no need to be perplexed any longer. And certainly any decent teacher will be expected *not* to be perplexed by this question any longer.

So here is Socrates in the *Meno*, still thinking of himself as a stingray, someone who numbs and perplexes others, but in the context of interrogating the slave-boy about a geometrical question, no longer thinking of himself as a *self-stinging* stingray, for he himself is certainly not perplexed about how the slave-boy ought to answer the questions he puts to him. This shift is a change of the very first importance.

A second point flows from the first. Part of the Paradox of Inquiry, we should remember, is that one who does not know what virtue is will not be able to aim the inquiry into what virtue is at the right target; that is, at virtue. But in questioning the slave-boy about how to construct a square with an area twice that of a given square, Socrates, being in full command of the right answer and also in charge of the questioning, can make sure the investigation is directed to the right target.

Readers of the *Meno* sometimes complain that Socrates, by the very way he interrogates the slave-boy, gives away the right answer to his question. (This is a common complaint from students who are reading Plato for the first time.) Perhaps there is some justice in that complaint. But the most fundamental point about this episode is that the slave-boy is brought to see *for himself* what the right answer is. That recognition, which Socrates interprets as recollecting knowledge his soul has brought with it to this life, is meant to back up the Theory of Recollection we discussed in the last chapter.

The Recollection Assumption, however, is only half of Socrates' response to the Paradox of Inquiry. The other part needed is something to deal with the problem about how one who does not know what virtue is can aim the inquiry *at the right target*. That issue is sidestepped in the slave-boy episode. Socrates, who *does* know the right answer, directs the inquiry and aims it at the correct target.

A third point is perhaps the most intriguing of all. In the passage above Socrates says of the slave-boy, 'Up to now, he thought he could speak well and fluently, on many occasions and before large audiences, on the subject of a square double the size of a given square . . .'. This remark parodies Meno's avowal of perplexity just a few pages earlier. Meno had said, 'Yet I have made many speeches about virtue before large audiences on a thousand occasions, very good speeches as I thought, but now I cannot even say what it is' (80b). Now Socrates attributes a parallel thought to the slave-boy.

It is hard to understand the parody as anything but a malicious joke. Meno is portrayed as a well-heeled young man of great promise, someone who has already studied with the Sophist, Gorgias, and could well have made speeches about virtue—if not literally 'on a thousand occasions', at least many times. The slave-boy is meant to be someone quite different. Socrates establishes that he speaks Greek. It could be that he is quite intelligent. But he is not of the right station in Athenian society to think he could 'speak well and fluently, on many occasions and before large audiences' on any subject. And even if he were, he would not think he could make such speeches on how to construct a square with an area twice that of a given square. This comment is a deliberate parody. But why? What is going on here?

If the *Meno* had ended with the stingray speeches by Meno and Socrates, it would count as an aporetic dialogue—a short one, to be sure, but a very powerful one with many features characteristic of the genre. The Paradox of Inquiry, which follows the stingray speeches, changes things radically. It calls Socratic inquiry into question and reveals that huge assumptions must be made if we are to be justified in thinking that such inquiry can move beyond perplexity to achieve positive results. The interrogation of the slave-boy is meant to buttress one of those assumptions. But, along the way, it makes fun of Meno's avowal of perplexity and, in this way, signals a certain impatience and dissatisfaction with aporetic dialogues. It seems that Plato is here having his character, Socrates, turn away from aporetic dialogues and move towards a form of dialogue that can be expected to produce positive results.

To be sure, the 'method of hypothesis' (*Meno* 86e) Socrates tries out in the latter part of the dialogue leads to only modest and tentative results. But some of the results are certainly positive. There is, perhaps most significantly, an attempt to say what knowledge is (97e–98a). It is the first attempt in Western philosophy to analyse knowledge as justified true belief, or true belief with an account (*logos*). Although that sort of analysis is much under attack these days, largely through the work of my colleague, Edmund Gettier, it has been, in the history of philosophy, a very popular attempt to say what it is to know something. Plato suggests this line of analysis again in the dialogue *Symposium* at 202a, and he suggests a different approach in book 7 of the *Republic*. But the discussion of knowledge in the latter part of the *Meno* remains one of Plato's important attempts to offer an account of what it is to know something.

Many Plato scholars think of the *Meno* as coming at or near the end of the early dialogues. In the dialogues usually assigned to the middle period, such as the *Phaedo*, the *Symposium*, and the *Republic*, there is no explicit display of shared perplexity. Socrates sometimes induces perplexity in his interlocutors, but he does not himself claim that he is equally perplexed by the matter under discussion. Indeed, he does not say that he is perplexed at all.

The matters under discussion in those dialogues are certainly deeply philosophical. In this respect they are quite unlike the interrogation of the slave-boy in the *Meno*. But Socrates is presented as moving along, through his questions, to positive conclusions. In this limited, but important, respect it is now made to seem that philosophy can be quite like geometry. Perhaps philosophy, too, has theorems, or something like them, that can be argued for and even proved.

Consider the *Phaedo*. This dialogue is often taken to offer the first explicit arguments for the grandest Platonic doctrine, the Theory of Forms. It also contains arguments for the immortality of the soul. So here are positive results of the first magnitude. But the only perplexity explicitly displayed in the dialogue *Phaedo* is *instrumental* perplexity, that is, perplexity that motivates someone to think through an issue or a line of reasoning and move to some positive conclusion. Moreover, it is not perplexity in which Socrates himself claims any share. Here is the passage:

'Come,' [Socrates] said, 'do you think there is something lacking in my argument? There are still many doubtful points and many objections for anyone who wants a thorough discussion of these matters. If you are discussing some other subject, I have nothing to say, but if you have some perplexity (*aporein*) about this one, do not hesitate to speak for yourselves and expound it if you think the argument could be improved, and if you think you will do better, take me along with you in the discussion.'

'I will tell you the truth, Socrates,' said Simmias. 'Both of us have been in perplexity (*aporōn*) for some time, and each of us has been urging the other to question you because we wanted to hear what you would say . . .' (*Phaedo* 84cd, Grube trans., somewhat modified)

Socrates tries to dispel Simmias' perplexity. He does so with what seems to be serene self-confidence. There is in this section of the *Phaedo* no suggestion of the self-stinging stingray.

Later on in the *Phaedo* there are at least vestiges of self-stinging perplexity, particularly in Socrates' 'autobiography'. Consider this passage, which I referred to in Chapter 3:

I will not even allow myself to say that where one is added to one either the one to which it is added or the one that is added becomes two, or that the one added and the one to which it is added becomes two because of the addition of the one to the other. I wonder (*thaumazō*) that, when each of them is separate from the other, each of them is one, nor are they then two, but that, when they come near to one another, this is the cause of their becoming two, the coming together and being placed close to one another. Nor can I any longer be persuaded that when one thing is divided, this division is the cause of its becoming two, for just now the cause of becoming two was the opposite. At the time it was their coming close together and one was added to the other, but now it is because one is taken and separated from the other. (96e–97b, Grube trans.)

This passage is part of Socrates' account of his search for causes, or explanations (*aitiai*). He wonders how putting one and one together could be what makes them, that is causes them to be, two, when, quite obviously they had to be two already, even before they were put together! And he wonders how division could be said to be what makes something two when the very opposite of division, namely, addition has just been said to make something two.

Although Socrates expresses diffidence about these matters, and although, when he advances his own theory of cause, or explanation, he calls it a 'second best' (99d) and only a 'safe but foolish' answer (100d), the vestiges of perplexity he has alluded to are clearly meant to give weight and force to his answer. The picture we are given is that, although there are lots of things here to be perplexed about, and Socrates has no doubt once been perplexed by all of them (and much more!), we must move on to at least a modest and tentative explanation of what makes something two, or tall, or beautiful. The explanation is, of course, that it is the relevant Form that makes a thing to be what it is. 'It is through Beauty [that is, through participating in the Form, Beauty] that beautiful things are made beautiful [. . .] and that it is through Bigness that big things are big and . . . smaller things are made small by Smallness' (100e–101a).

Two points are worth special emphasis. First, Socrates does not present himself as being currently perplexed about these matters. To be sure, he is somewhat tentative about his conclusions. He expresses the desire to say more. But he is certainly not in the numbing grip of perplexity. Second, the perplexity he alludes to, but does not himself express, is instrumental to supporting his theory, the Theory of Forms. The idea is that other theories of 'causality' threaten to produce perplexity. His theory, even though, as so far developed, it offers only limited satisfaction, is free of the perplexities that burden its rivals.

What about other dialogues of the middle period? What about, for example, the *Republic*? One might have expected to find shared perplexity in book 1 of Plato's *Republic*. After all, that work is usually taken by Plato scholars to be, in effect, an early dialogue that Plato never brought out separately but later recycled as the opening book in his great work on justice. Certainly the style of book 1 is much more like that of the early dialogues. And the book does end with Socrates claiming ignorance about what justice is.

A close look at book 1 of the *Republic* reveals, however, a work that is very different from the early aporetic dialogues. Many of the major claims of the later books of the *Republic* are already sketched in book 1. To be sure, they are not developed fully in this book, and they are certainly not fully argued for there. But the very substantial structure of the work as a whole is already adumbrated in its first book.

Moreover, the expected profession of Socratic ignorance, which is to be found at the very end of book 1 (354bc), far from being a confession of mind-numbing perplexity, is almost a stylized gesture, best understood as an admission that the ideas Socrates has thrown out need much more development and defence. And nowhere in book 1 does either Socrates, or one of his interlocutors, say he is in perplexity.

In book 2 Glaucon, one of Socrates' interlocutors, says he is perplexed about what Thrasymachus and others have said in the earlier book (358c). Socrates uses his perplexity to motivate the discussion. There are no more avowals of perplexity by anyone, by either Socrates or his interlocutors, in the whole work.

In book 6 Socrates at one point says the soul is perplexed about the good (505e) and in book 7 Socrates clearly extols the instrumental value of perplexity. First he says that the soul is puzzled about a report from the senses that something is hard, when the soul also gets a report that the thing is soft, or that something is both heavy and light (524a). He seems to have in mind the familiar claim that something may be hard in this respect, or at this time, but also soft in that respect, or at that time, and similarly with light and heavy. At the end of that page Socrates says this:

> But if something opposite to it is always seen at the same time, so that nothing is apparently any more one than the opposite of one, then something would be needed to judge the matter. The soul would then be perplexed (*aporein*), would look for an answer, would stir up its understanding, and would ask what the one itself is. And so this would be among the subjects that lead the soul and turn it around towards the study of that which is. (524e–525a, Grube trans.)

The 'study of that which is' mentioned here, is the study of the Forms. Socrates' idea is that being perplexed about how something in the sensible world can be both F and the opposite of F can lead the soul's understanding to the Forms. The Forms, he thinks, are not what they are merely with a qualification; they are unqualifiedly whatever they are. Thus the Form, Beauty, is simply beautiful and never, in any respect or at any time, ugly.

So here is a clear acknowledgement of the instrumental value of perplexity. Equally clearly, this instrumental perplexity is something to be got beyond. One who has come to make a distinction between sensible particulars and the Forms will no longer be surprised or perplexed that sensible particulars are both hard and soft, light and heavy. Having its lightness or heaviness qualified by time and respect is part of what it is for something to be a sensible particular. We should expect nothing else. There is no cause to be perplexed about this matter any more.

8

Second-Order Perplexity: *Parmenides*

THE reason, we should recall, that Socrates in book 7 of the *Republic* had not been at all puzzled about how something could seem to be both hard and soft, or light and heavy, is that Socrates had learned to distinguish the Forms themselves from the things that participate in them. Thus he had learned to distinguish hardness ('the hard itself') and softness ('the soft itself') from the various things in this world of coming-to-be and passing-away, such as loaves of bread— things that are now soft and later hard as a rock, or, like a bed, hard in one part, say, its frame and soft in another, say, its mattress. The notion seemed to be that hard or soft things in the sensible world, being only reflections of the Forms, are for that reason only imperfectly hard or soft, whereas the Form, hardness, is perfectly hard, and the Form, softness, perfectly soft. Once we are clear about this distinction, we are to be no longer perplexed about how sensible things can be both hard and soft, or now one and now the other.

Perhaps Plato's mood of self-satisfaction at being able to resolve perplexity with his Theory of Forms affected his philosophical attitudes more generally. Gregory Vlastos suggests as much when he writes about Plato this way:

When he first projects a new theory that succeeds in solving to his immediate satisfaction hitherto unsolved problems and satisfies deep longings of his heart, delight in his creation may produce a kind of rapture that leaves little room for self-questioning. This is Plato's mood in the *Phaedo*, the *Symposium*, and the *Republic*. The theory of forms is then the greatest of certainties, a place of unshakable security to which he may retreat when doubtful or perplexed about anything else.[1]

[1] Vlastos (1954), 342.

Alas! the 'place of unshakeable security' showed itself to be a highly exposed place of great vulnerability.

In Plato's dialogue *Parmenides* a surprisingly young Socrates is made to present, explain, and try to defend Plato's Theory of Forms in the face of relentless cross-examination by the Presocratic philosopher Parmenides. We don't know whether the historical Socrates ever actually met the historical Parmenides. In fact, we can't even be sure their lives overlapped sufficiently for such a meeting to have taken place. But even if Socrates did meet Parmenides in real life, he would certainly not have been in a position to defend Plato's Theory of Forms, something that Plato did not develop until well into the next century. So, whatever we come to say about the historical authenticity of the figure of Socrates in Plato's early dialogues, we must agree that the young Socrates in this dialogue is a stand-in for Plato in Plato's own self-critical examination of his most ambitious philosophical theory.

As the dialogue opens Socrates proudly disarms puzzles of the hard-soft variety by appeal to the Theory of Forms. He tells Parmenides' disciple, Zeno, that there is nothing astonishing about the fact that some things are both equal and unequal, or both one and many. (This would be like sensible things being both hard and soft, thick and thin.) However, if someone could show, he says,

that the kinds (*genē*) and forms (*eidē*) themselves have in themselves these opposite properties, that would call for astonishment (*thaumazein*). But if someone should demonstrate [only] that I am one thing and many, what's astonishing about that? He will say, when he wants to show that I am many, that my right side is different from my left, and my front from my back, and likewise with my upper and lower parts—since I take it I do partake of multitude. But when he wants to show that I am one, he will say I'm one person among the seven of us, because I also partake of oneness. Thus he shows that both are true.   (129cd, Gill/Ryan trans.)

As if deliberately recalling the argument for Forms at *Phaedo* 74ab, the argument that begins with the observation that there are sticks and stones that appear both equal and unequal and leads to the conclusion that there is something perfectly equal, Socrates then goes on at 129d to talk about sticks and stones that can be both many and one, even though the one itself (that is, the Form, unity) is certainly not many, any more than the Form, plurality, can be one.

'I would be much more impressed,' Socrates goes on to tell Zeno,

if someone were able to show this same perplexity (*tēn autēn tautēn aporian*), which you and Parmenides have spelled out in the case of visible things, is also similarly involved in the various ways in the forms themselves—in things grasped by reasoning.   (129e–130a, Gill/Ryan trans.)

Parmenides takes up Socrates' challenge. He doesn't exactly show that 'this same perplexity' is involved in the Forms themselves. That is, he doesn't try to show that the Form, the F itself, is both F and not F. But he does show that the perplexities that afflict the Forms are at least as serious and at least as baffling as those that plague things in the sensible world of coming-to-be and passing-away.

Parmenides first gets Socrates to express puzzlement about which things there are Forms for, a puzzlement that betrays the fact that several distinct lines of reasoning have led to positing Forms in the first place. The worry is that, whereas one line of reasoning yields one domain for the Forms, another line of reasoning may yield quite a different domain, perhaps one that includes the first domain and more, or one that is included by it, or only overlaps it. Here is the way the passage goes:

'Socrates,' [Parmenides] said, 'you are much to be admired for your keenness for argument! Tell me. Have you yourself distinguished as separate, in the way you mention, certain forms themselves, and also as separate the things that partake of them? And do you think that likeness is itself something, separate from the likeness we have? And one and many and all the things you heard Zeno read about a while ago?'

'I do indeed', Socrates answered.

'And what about these?' asked Parmenides. 'Is there a form itself by itself, of just, and beautiful, and good, and everything of that sort?'

'Yes', he said.

'What about a form of human being, separate from us and all those like us? Is there a form itself of human being, or fire, or water?'

Socrates said, 'Parmenides, I have often found myself in perplexity (*en aporia*) as to whether I should talk about those in the same way as the others, or differently.'

'And what about these, Socrates? Things that might seem absurd, like hair and mud and filth, or anything else totally undignified and worthless? Are you perplexed (*aporeis*) as to whether or not you should say that there is a separate form for each of these too, which in turn is other than anything we can touch with our hands?'

'Not at all,' Socrates answered. 'In these cases, the things are just the things we see; it would surely be too absurd to suppose that they have a form. All the same, I have sometimes been troubled by a doubt whether what is true in one case may not be true in all . . .' (130b–d, Gill/Ryan and Cornford trans., modified)

Readers of this passage may well suffer from their own *aporia* in simply trying to understand this passage. Why should Socrates hesitate to say that there are Forms for human being, or for fire, or for water? After all, the idea of there being a Form for human being, that is, for 'man' (*anthrōpos*), is often taken to be a paradigmatically Platonic thesis.

Presumably readers are meant to realize that there is something crucial about 'incomplete' or 'relative' notions, such as that of being equal, or unequal, like, or unlike, that does not hold at all for the notion of being a human being. Thus Socrates' claim that something in the perceptible world that is equal, or like, can also be seen to be, at another time or in another respect, unequal and unlike is plausible enough. But the parallel claim for human being does not seem equally plausible.[2] It seems, that is, that there are some perfectly good samples of human being—not beings that are human ones at this time only, or in this respect only, but simply human beings. About them we are not tempted to make a contrast between the merely qualified humanness of human beings in the sensible world and the unqualified humanness of the Form, human being.

In fact, Plato had had Socrates make a point quite similar to this one about fingers in book 7 of the *Republic*. Here is the passage:

These, we say, are three fingers—the smallest, the second, and the middle finger. . . . It's apparent that each of them is equally a finger, and it makes no difference in this regard whether the finger is seen to be in the middle or at either end, whether it is dark or pale, thick or thin, or anything else of that sort, for in all these cases, an ordinary soul isn't compelled to ask the understanding what a finger is, since sight doesn't suggest to it that a finger is at the same time the opposite of a finger. (523cd, Grube trans.)

[2] See G. E. L. Owen's discussion of this point in his 'A Proof in the Peri Ideōn', in Owen (1986), esp. pp. 172–7.

The same is true for human being (man, *anthrōpos*). Whether my friend is light or dark, blonde or red-headed, tall or short, she is not both a human being and the opposite of a human being. So knowing what a human being is can be, it is plausible to think, simply knowing what she unqualifiedly is. We needn't suppose that there is a separate Form of human being just to keep what it is to be a human being uncontaminated from its opposite.

Similar worries apply to fire and water. Of course, we may find it more difficult to locate uncontaminated samples of water (no doubt even more difficult today than in Plato's time!), or unqualified samples of fire. But there are such things. And so, again, the search for something perfectly F might not lead us to Forms in the case of fire and water either.

What about hair, mud, and filth? Why should Socrates have been inclined actually to deny that there are Forms for these things—not just be in perplexity about whether there are Forms in these cases but rather be inclined, without perplexity, simply to deny that there are Forms in these cases? 'In these cases, the things are just the things we see,' he says; 'it would surely be too absurd (*atopon*) to suppose that they have a Form' (130d). The point about there being unqualified samples of them—that is, hair, for example, that is simply hair and in no way the opposite of hair (whatever exactly that might be!), seems to apply here as well. But, beyond finding the appeal to Forms unnecessary, Socrates is inclined to dismiss as absurd the suggestion that there might be Forms for hair, mud, and filth? Why this strong reaction?

We aren't told why. But I suspect that the relevant consideration this time is the normative implication of the Theory of Forms.[3] Plato tends to suppose that things in this world strive to be like the Forms, and that it is a good thing that they do. Even the equal sticks and stones Socrates talks about in the *Phaedo* are said to 'strive to be like the Equal', though they fall short of this goal (75a). One supposes it would be ludicrous to him that anything might strive to be like ideal

---

[3] Constance Meinwald makes a related suggestion: '. . . he wants his forms to be glorious entities and would naturally feel this to be incompatible with being muddy. Yet the superexemplification view must take the form, Mud, to be some supremely muddy thing' (Meinwald (1991), 165).

hair, or ideal mud, let alone ideal filth, and even more ridiculous that it should be good that things so strive.

Yet Socrates is perplexed, for he adds, 'I have sometimes been troubled by a doubt whether what is true in one case may not be true in all.' What is nagging at Socrates here is presumably an obvious implication of what Aristotle calls the 'one-over-many argument' (*Metaphysics* 1. 9, 990ᵇ13), which is perhaps most clearly referred to in book 10 of Plato's *Republic*:

> We are in the habit of assuming one Form for each multiplicity of things (*peri hekasta ta polla*) to which we give the same name.   (596a)

According to this line of thought, so long as there are many things to which we apply the term 'hair', there will be a form for hair. And the same will hold for 'mud' and 'filth'.

So here is a major difficulty with the Theory of Forms. The lines of reasoning that lead Plato to conclude that there are Forms are various. And the domain of Forms that one line of reasoning leads to may be quite different from the domain suggested by a different line of reasoning.

There follows in the *Parmenides* a bewildering array of puzzles about what the relation of participation alleged to obtain between Forms and particulars can consist in. Does each thing that participates in a Form receive 'as its share' the Form as a whole, or only a part of it (131a)? If as a whole, then each Form as a whole will be, as a whole, in each thing that participates in it and so will thus be separate from itself, which seems unacceptable (131b). If only as a part, then many other absurdities threaten. For example, there will be the absurdity that only a small part of Largeness will be needed to make some particular object large (131d).

Characteristically in the middle dialogues Plato makes Socrates express diffidence about the exact nature of participation. Thus in the *Phaedo* at 100d Socrates says that nothing else makes something beautiful 'other than the presence of, or the sharing in, or however you may describe its relationship to that Beautiful we mentioned'. In the *Parmenides* Socrates is made to face up to the difficulty about saying just what participation actually is.

Parmenides goes on in the dialogue to raise the most famous difficulty of all for Plato's Theory of Forms, namely, what has come to be called 'the Third Man Argument' (132ab). It is, in fact, an indefinite regress of 'largenesses', rather than of 'men', that the argument threatens, a point that is relevant to the earlier worry about the domain of the Forms. Socrates expresses no hesitation at all about supposing that there is a Form, largeness (or 'the large itself'), over any grouping of large things, something that makes each of these large things large. But when Parmenides notes that Socrates also wants to say of this Form that it, too, is large, he makes a new grouping—the original set of large particulars plus the Form, largeness, and applies the One-Over-Many Principle to this new grouping to establish a new, higher-level Form of largeness. Since this move can be repeated ad infinitum, Parmenides is able to present Socrates with the unwelcome conclusion, 'So there will no longer be one Form for you in each case, but countless many' (132b).

Much of the recent discussion of the Third Man Argument is either a direct or an indirect response to a seminal article Gregory Vlastos published in 1954. In his article Vlastos suggested that this argument, and the others surrounding it in the *Parmenides*, are a 'record of honest perplexity'. What the Vlastos-inspired discussion soon revealed, however, is that Plato's argument not only expresses Plato's own perplexity, it also induces perplexity of its own. That discussion revealed that the premiss set Vlastos had used to reconstruct the Third Man is inconsistent. Since from inconsistent premisses anything follows, the argument as reconstructed by Vlastos cannot be thought to yield specifically the unwanted conclusion that 'There is not just one Form in each case, but countless many', any more than it yields the contradictory of that conclusion. So now there is a fresh perplexity about how Plato's argument could seem to establish a certain unwanted conclusion when, apparently, it could be used equally well to establish the opposite conclusion.

Wilfrid Sellars, S. Marc Cohen, and others have offered reconstructions of the Third Man passage that use a consistent premiss set to yield the unwanted conclusion.[4] The difficulties they had to surmount to accomplish this task serve to underscore the difficulties that being clear about Plato's Theory of Forms presents.

[4] Sellars (1955) and Cohen (1971*b*).

After the Third Man Argument, Parmenides offers another, unwelcome, regress argument to threaten the unity of the Forms and then moves on to offer an argument for the conclusion that the Forms, even if they exist, will be unknowable. He says that this perplexity is the greatest of all, though, he adds, there are many more (133b).

Part I of the *Parmenides* then ends with the following exchange, which brings out the seriousness of these 'second-order perplexities' but which also makes clear how reluctant Socrates is to give up the Theory of Forms, despite the flaws:

'And yet, Socrates,' Parmenides went on, 'these difficulties and many more besides are inevitably involved in the Forms, if these characters of things really exist, and one is going to distinguish each form as a thing just by itself. The result is that the hearer is perplexed (*aporein*) and inclined either to question their existence, or to contend that, if they do exist, they must certainly be unknowable by our human nature . . .'

'I admit that, Parmenides. I quite agree with what you are saying.'

'But on the other hand,' Parmenides continued, 'if, in view of all these difficulties and others like them, one refuses to admit that Forms of things exist or to distinguish a definite Form in every case, one will have nothing on which to fix one's thought . . . and in so doing one will completely destroy the significance of all discourse.'   (135a–c, Cornford trans., modified)

What we see in part I of the dialogue *Parmenides* is thus that perplexity continues to animate philosophy. The aporetic dialogues had shown perplexity as an instigator of philosophical investigation. In the *Phaedo* and in the *Republic* Socrates had suggested that a philosophical theory, the Theory of Forms, might alleviate perplexity. In those dialogues Socrates does not himself own up to being perplexed about any of the matters that perplex others. After all, he has the Theory of Forms.

Now in the *Parmenides*, after Parmenides has produced a dazzling display of perplexity-inducing difficulties with the Theory of Forms, Socrates admits to what I am calling 'second-order perplexity', perplexity about a philosophical theory conceived in response to first-order perplexity. Yet Parmenides also encourages Socrates not to give up on the theory by reminding him of the real value of the theory.

What was Plato's own response to this situation? Scholars are divided on the question of what happens to the Theory of Forms in Plato's later writings. In her recent paper 'Good-bye to the Third Man', in the *Cambridge Companion to Plato*,[5] Constance Meinwald summarizes the situation nicely. According to one line of interpretation, she tells us, Plato suffered 'a major crisis in which he attacked and actually destroyed the theory that was his masterpiece' and 'spent his last years in extensive critical activity', the later dialogues of Plato being only 'a record of this barren final period'.[6]

According to a second line of interpretation, Meinwald goes on to say, the Theory of Forms is 'a hopelessly flawed creation, whose hopelessness was realized by Plato himself in the *Parmenides*' in such a way that Plato 'was then in a position to do some good philosophy in the late period'.[7] This line of interpretation, Meinwald says, gained its greatest impetus from Gilbert Ryle.

As her own alternative to these two stories, Meinwald suggests the following:

I believe that Plato composed the first part of the *Parmenides* in order to exhibit where his middle-period description of Forms needed development. . . . The *Parmenides* as a whole gives the best possible evidence for Plato's response to the problems it introduces . . . the dialogue shows that his response was successful. As the late period began, the theory of Forms was in new leaf.[8]

If Meinwald is correct, then second-order perplexity is for Plato an impetus to further philosophical inquiry. The relief from perplexity had been, it now seems, only temporary.[9]

---

[5] Kraut (1992), 365–96.   [6] Ibid. 390.   [7] Ibid.   [8] Ibid. 391.
[9] Cf. David Bostock's account of this development in Bostock (1988), 13–14.

Professionalized Perplexity: The Midwife

THE writings of Plato give us three memorable images of Socrates. In the *Apology* Socrates describes himself as 'a kind of gadfly' for 'a great and noble horse', Athens, which, he says, needs to be stirred up (30e). In the *Meno*, as we have seen, Socrates' interlocutor characterizes him as a stingray who 'makes anyone who comes close and touches it feel numb' and unable to speak (80a). Socrates, as I have emphasized, accepts the stingray image, provided that the stingray also stings itself, for, as he insists, he is himself as numb and perplexed as those he interrogates. The implication is clearly that some of the same questions that numb and perplex Socrates' interlocutors also numb and perplex him. So the second image of Socrates is that of the self-stinging stingray.

In the dialogue *Theaetetus* we get a third, equally memorable, image. There Socrates says he is an intellectual midwife. Here are parts of the long passage in which he explains what he means by this image:

SOCRATES: . . . People say that I am a very odd sort of person, always causing people to get into perplexity (*aporein*). You must have heard that, surely?

THEAETETUS: Yes, I have.

SOCRATES: And shall I tell you what is the explanation of that?

THEAETETUS: Yes, please do.

SOCRATES: Well, if you will just think of the general facts about the business of midwifery, you will see more easily what I mean. You know, I suppose, that women never practise as midwives while they are still conceiving and bearing children themselves. . . . it is the midwives who can tell better than anyone else whether women are pregnant or not. . . . And then it is the midwives who have the power to bring on the pains, and also, if they think fit, to relieve them; they do it by the use of simple drugs, and by singing incantations. In difficult cases, too, they can bring about the birth; or, if they consider it advisable, they can promote a miscarriage.

(149a–d)

SOCRATES: Now my art of midwifery is just like theirs in most respects. The difference is that I attend men and not women, and that I watch over the labour of their souls, not of their bodies. And the most important thing about my art is the ability to apply all possible tests to the offspring, to determine whether the young mind is being delivered of a phantom, that is, an error, or a fertile truth. For one thing I have in common with the ordinary midwives is that I myself am barren of wisdom. The common reproach against me is that I am always asking questions of other people but never express my own views about anything, because there is no wisdom in me; and that is true enough. And the reason of it is this, that God compels me to attend the travail of others, but has forbidden me to procreate. So that I am not in any sense a wise man; I cannot claim as the child of my own soul any discovery worth the name of wisdom. But with those who associate with me it is different. At first some of them may give the impression of being ignorant and stupid; but as time goes on and our association continues, all whom God permits are seen to make progress—a progress that is amazing both to other people and to themselves. And yet it is clear that this is not due to anything they have learnt from me; it is that they discover within themselves a multitude of beautiful things, which they bring forth into light. But it is I, with God's help, who deliver them of this offspring.

(150b–d)

[SOCRATES:] There is another point also in which those who associate with me are like women in child-birth. They suffer the pains of labour, and are filled day and night with perplexity; indeed they suffer far more than women. And this pain my art is able to bring on, and also to allay.

(151a, Levett trans., slightly altered)

These three images—the gadfly, the self-stinging stingray, and the midwife—are essential parts of Plato's successive efforts to get at what was so special about his own teacher, Socrates. They are also crucial parts of Plato's successive efforts to say what a philosopher is, and what philosophy is.

Suppose that, of Plato's writings, only the *Apology* were extant. What sort of picture of Socrates would we have? More specifically, what could we understand Socrates to mean when he characterizes himself as a gadfly to Athens?

The gadfly image certainly fits well with the Socratic maxim, also from the *Apology*, 'The unexamined life is not worth living' (38a). We could learn from the *Apology* that Socrates thought most of his fellow citizens were unreflective about their lives and that they made as if they knew and understood things they did not really know or understand. Socrates, the gadfly, stung them into a recognition that their pretensions to knowledge were highly problematic.

Socrates' claim that he himself knows nothing is, of course, also prominent in the *Apology*. So we have in that work the picture of someone who questions others, not from a position of assumed knowledge, but rather from a position of self-confessed ignorance. This point might suggest the idea that Socrates asked people, not just about matters that everyone considers difficult, but precisely about matters that most people think too simple and basic for a grown person to question. Reflection on that suggestion might lead, in turn, to the thought that philosophy, as practised by Socrates anyway, concerns itself with matters that most people consider too simple and too basic for a grown-up to raise questions about.

From the *Apology* alone, however, one could hardly get the idea that perplexity is important to philosophy, or even that it was important for Socrates. To be sure, there is nothing in that work to *rule out* the idea that Socrates' claim of ignorance might be based upon a profound perplexity, or that his questioning of others might have induced perplexity in them. But perplexity is not displayed or talked about in the *Apology*. And we readers are given no direct indication that the kinds of question that preoccupied Socrates concerned matters that are problematic in ways that naturally, perhaps even inevitably, produce perplexity.

Perplexity is first displayed and discussed in other early dialogues, such as the *Laches*, which we discussed in Chapter 3, and the *Euthyphro*, which we took up in Chapter 4. It is those aporetic dialogues that prepare us for the image of the stingray in the *Meno*. In the *Charmides*, which is also an early aporetic dialogue, there is this memorable passage in which perplexity is said to be easily passed on to others, like a yawn:

[SOCRATES:] Critias heard me say this, and saw that I was in perplexity (*aporounta*), and as one person, when another yawns in his presence, catches the yawning from him, so did he seem driven into perplexities (*aporias*) by my perplexity (*hup' emou aporountos*). But as he had a reputation to maintain, he was ashamed to admit before the company that he could not answer my challenge or determine the question at issue, and he made an unintelligible attempt to hide his perplexity (*aporian*).

(169cd, Jowett trans., slightly altered)

Just as one covers one's mouth when one yawns in response to the yawning of another, so Critias tried to conceal the perplexity he caught from Socrates.

The image of the stingray goes well beyond the idea of yawning a contagious and somewhat embarrassing yawn. For one thing, it is a much more hostile image! It includes the idea that Socrates makes his otherwise perfectly articulate interlocutors numb, baffled, even speechless. He does this by getting them to realize that they are not able to explain, or give an account of, something they had previously thought they understood very well.

Now of course being questioned in a way that makes obvious one doesn't know or understand something one had thought one knew or understood, perhaps had been expected to know or understand, may be shaming in a way that makes one numb, perplexed, even speechless. This is true regardless of the subject under discussion. So the picture of Socrates as a consummately clever questioner who can reduce his interlocutors to confusion and perplexity does not, so far, mark off anything special about philosophy. What changes things is that Socrates, the questioner, is also perplexed. He is perplexed despite the fact that (1) the matter under discussion is very basic, (2) Socrates may well have questioned others, perhaps many others, about this same matter, and (3) he has presumably reflected on it himself, perhaps on many different occasions.

So when Socrates, in the *Meno*, accepts the stingray image only on condition that the stingray stings itself, he emphasizes a feature of Socratic questioning that is peculiarly philosophical. In philosophy, even the seasoned investigator may still be perplexed—and not, now, because he had believed that he knew the answers to such basic questions and was shamed into the realization that he didn't, but even though he didn't think he knew the answers and had already tried to come up with answers on many earlier occasions.

The speechlessness characteristic of someone who is stung with a genuinely philosophical perplexity is also revealed to be of a special kind. It is not merely the speechlessness of shame at having one's incompetence revealed. It is a paralysis that undermines one's confidence that one even knows how to use the language. After all, if one can't give a satisfactory account of what virtue is, what right has one to assume that one even knows how to use the word, 'virtue' (*aretē*), correctly?

The self-stinging stingray is thus a much richer image than that of the gadfly, at least as the gadfly is used in the *Apology*. Commensurately, it suggests a much richer story about what philosophy is. Philosophy, it now seems, is, or includes, an inquiry into matters so basic to the meanings of common words that, when one meets with even temporary failure, one's confidence that one even understands everyday words and expressions may be undermined.

What now about the midwife image? How does it differ from that of the self-stinging stingray?

Certainly the midwife image includes the idea of inducing perplexity. Perplexity is now portrayed as the labour of philosophical childbirth. But there are several features of the midwife image that make it significantly different from the stingray image and that are especially worth commenting on. One thing is the aim of midwifery. Midwives exist to aid in childbirth. This is their primary purpose. Presumably philosophical midwives also exist to aid in philosophical childbirth, where philosophical childbirth is presumably the delivery of a viable philosophical theory, doctrine, or analysis. This feature of the midwife image guarantees Socrates a more positive and productive role than we could possibly get from the stingray image.

Socrates includes in the midwiferic responsibilities he details the inducement of miscarriage, that is, abortion, as well as the diagnosis of false pregnancies, which result in what he calls mere 'windeggs'. So a secondary function of the philosophic midwife consists in the identification of unviable and merely sham theories, doctrines, and analyses. Again, this feature goes well beyond anything we could gather about philosophy, or about Socrates, from the stingray image.

Most important of all, the midwife image delineates two distinct, philosophical roles. Socrates clearly thinks of his interlocutor—in this dialogue it is the brilliant boy mathematician, Theaetetus—as doing philosophy. It is the interlocutor who is pregnant, or is thought to be so. Ideally the interlocutor will give birth to some viable philosophical result. By contrast, Socrates, the philosophical midwife, has been forbidden by God from procreating. He is barren and he has agreed not even to try to become pregnant. His role is therefore an enabling and critical one, kept deliberately distinct from that of the would-be producer of philosophical offspring.[1]

In deploying the image of the philosophical midwife, Plato has found a way to honour Socrates and his philosophical barrenness without suggesting that the role of Socrates exhausts philosophy. Socrates is the ideal critic in philosophy, someone who can induce the labour of perplexity when it is appropriate, can alleviate it when appropriate, can identify unviable theories, doctrines, and analyses, and is not in competition to produce the best-looking philosophical baby.

All of us with professional training and experience in philosophy know philosophers who are Socratic midwives, in accordance with the image Plato gives us in the *Theaetetus*. That is, we know philosophers who are excellent critics, imaginative generators of thought experiments, hypotheses, counter-examples, and distinctions, but who themselves never give birth to any books, perhaps not even to many published articles. They may become famous for a criticism, or a refutation, perhaps published somewhere, perhaps only passed down by philosophical legend, but they have no theory or doctrine or analysis to their name. A philosophy department is much better off for having a good philosophical midwife in its ranks. But the

---

[1] R. G. Wengert thinks that the midwife image, as Socrates applies it to himself, is inconsistent. On the one hand, Socrates says that midwives, though past the child-bearing age, need to have had the experience of having borne children to be good midwives ('. . . human nature is too weak to acquire skill in matters of which it has no experience'—149c). On the other hand, Socrates insists that he has never himself been philosophically pregnant ('God compels me to be a midwife, but has prevented me from giving birth. So I'm not at all wise myself, and there hasn't been any discovery of that kind born to me as the offspring of my mind'—150cd). (Wengert (1988)) but see Burnyeat (1977), n. 6.)

whole enterprise of doing philosophy would come to a grinding halt if there were only midwives in our philosophy departments. Some philosophers need to be genuinely pregnant, and to have babies. The midwife image in the *Theaetetus* marks off a role of special importance for a philosopher who, so to speak, specializes in inducing perplexity in such a way that this specialty can be aimed at helping produce viable results—philosophical theories, or doctrines or analyses. Socratic perplexity can be given full honours without suggesting either that it is all there is to philosophy, or that it is something that we all must aim at getting over, or getting beyond.

As already noted, Theaetetus is introduced to Socrates as a brilliant boy mathematician by his teacher, Theodorus. A reader familiar only with the early aporetic dialogues will not be at all surprised to find Socrates directing his questioning efforts at a young person. Good examples of this Socratic practice include the dialogue *Charmides*, from which we took the yawning image, and the dialogue *Lysis*, in which two youngsters explore with Socrates what it is to be a friend. But a reader of book 7 of the *Republic*, where Socrates condemns doing philosophy with young people,[2] may be puzzled at Socrates' rekindled interest in youth. Here is the *Republic* passage:

And isn't it one lasting precaution not to let them taste arguments while they're young? I don't suppose that it has escaped your notice then, when young people get their first taste of arguments, they misuse it by treating it as a kind of game of contradiction. They imitate those who've refuted them by refuting others themselves, and, like puppies, they enjoy dragging and tearing those around them with their arguments. (539ab, Grube trans.)[3]

The return to philosophy for the youth is made explicit by this speech of Theodorus:

---

[2] Alexander Nehamas appeals to this point to provide evidence for supposing that, in the early dialogues, Plato at least intends to give an accurate picture of the historical Socrates: 'That in his middle and late works Plato is willing to criticize Socrates, often through the persona of Socrates himself, is one indication that in his earlier works he *does* try to represent Socrates as he genuinely sees him to be, whether or not we can trust his representation to be accurate' (Nehamas (1992), 281–2 n. 11).

[3] See Alexander Nehamas's discussion of the way Plato has Socrates, in the *Republic*, in effect, criticize and condemn the historical Socrates for corrupting the youth of Athens (Nehamas (1992), 281–2).

But do make one of the young people answer you. I am not used to this kind of discussion, and I'm too old to get into the way of it. But it would be suitable enough for them and they would profit more by it.   (146b, Levett trans.)

Later on in the dialogue Socrates makes clear the conditions under which he approves of doing philosophy with young people. 'Do not be unjust in your questions,' he admonishes Theaetetus:

it is the height of unreasonableness that a person who professes to care for moral goodness should be consistently unjust in discussion. I mean by injustice . . . the behavior of a man who does not take care to keep controversy distinct from discussion; a man who forgets that in controversy he may play about and trip up his opponent as often as he can, but that in discussion he must be serious, he must keep on helping his opponent to his feet again, and point out to him only those of his slips which are due to himself or to the intellectual society which he has previously frequented. If you observe this distinction, those who associate with you will blame themselves for their confusion and their difficulties (*aporias*), not you. They will seek your company, and think of you as their friend; but they will loathe themselves, and seek refuge from themselves in philosophy . . . But if you follow the common practice and do the opposite, you will get the opposite results. Instead of philosophers, you will make your companions grow up to be the enemies of philosophy.   (167e–168b, Levett trans.)

This passage seems to present a direct response to the one at the end of *Republic* 7. There, following the description of young people making arguments into a mere game of contradiction, Socrates had warned of dire consequences:

Then, when they've refuted many and been refuted by them in turn, they forcefully and quickly fall into disbelieving what they believed before. And, as a result, they themselves and the whole of philosophy are discredited in the eyes of others.   (539bc, Grube trans.)

In the *Theaetetus* Socrates repeats the warning: 'Instead of philosophers, you will make your companions grow up to be the enemies of philosophy.' But he now targets specifically those who are 'consistently unjust in discussion'. By contrast, those who have been dealt with justly will, Socrates says, 'seek refuge from themselves in philosophy'.

The teacher of mine who most closely fitted the Socratic midwife image also conformed to these Socratic strictures against being 'unjust in discussion'. I can remember occasions when he presented devastating objections to a line of thought that I, or one of my fellow students, was trying to develop. Just at the point at which we felt thoroughly humiliated, he would frown in deep reflection and suggest, 'But perhaps what you wanted to say was this.' There would then follow an imaginatively generous and resourceful interpretation of what we had tried to say, an interpretation so sophisticated that we would be only too eager to embrace it and claim it as our own. Of course, even that more sophisticated suggestion might eventually fall victim to later criticism. But, if so, it would not be from what Plato here calls 'unjust questions', but rather from faults that we would be able to see, by then, made it altogether worthy of rejection.

For many of us students of philosophy, it is perhaps the teacher who was a midwife to us, rather than the one who was just a stingray, or even the one who was a brilliant procreator of his own ideas, who has made the greatest impact on our lives. We cannot know whether Plato's own teacher, Socrates, ever practised 'live' midwifery on his most illustrious pupil. But the recollected Socrates seems to have acted as a midwife for Plato throughout his long and preternaturally productive life. Yet it was not until he wrote his dialogue *Theaetetus* that he was able to claim this memorable image for his unforgettable teacher.

10

Perplexity as Itself a Target of Inquiry

PLATO'S dialogue *Theaetetus* ends with an agreement to meet again the next day. His dialogue *Sophist* seems to offer an account of the next day's meeting. The main characters from the *Theaetetus*— Socrates, Theodorus, and Theodorus' pupil, Theaetetus—are on hand for the discussion in the *Sophist*. But Socrates steps aside to let a newcomer, the Eleatic Stranger, take over the role of discussion leader. Why?

Scholars have suggested various explanations for the displacement of Socrates in this dialogue. Gilbert Ryle maintained that the dialogues were written for dramatic presentation and that Plato insisted on playing the part of Socrates. When he became unable to play that part, Ryle speculated, Plato had Socrates withdraw from the proceedings and turn them over to another character, the Eleatic Stranger. In conversation Ryle even suggested that Plato had lost his teeth and, for that reason, was shy about appearing in public. In his book *Plato's Progress* Ryle offered the more modest speculation that Plato had become ill and, on that account, was unable to play Socrates in public.[1]

My discussion of the midwife image in the last chapter suggests a different explanation. Socrates as midwife is an expert at inducing the labour of philosophical perplexity. Yet, as I emphasized in the last chapter, midwifery is clearly aimed at childbirth. One implication of the midwife image is then that Socrates, the relentless questioner, can be given full honours without implying that his role exhausts philosophy. In fact, his role would be indefensible, if there were not pregnant thinkers capable of giving birth to viable philosophical theories and analyses. What happens then in the *Sophist* is

---

[1] (Cambridge University Press, 1966), 28.

that Plato retires Socrates so that he can present a way of doing philosophy quite distinct from midwiferic cross-examination.[2] There are already signs in the *Theaetetus* that Plato wants to move beyond the idea of philosophy as midwifery and childbirth. Perhaps he doesn't see how to fit some of his philosophical interests into the obstetrical analogy. He needs another model for what it is to do philosophy, but he comes up with nothing else. Thus, as Myles Burnyeat points out, 'reminders of the comparison between the Socratic method and the midwife's art recur at intervals throughout Part I [151e, 157cd, 160e–161b, 161e, 184b] but not again until the brief concluding remarks which bring the dialogue to a close [210bd]'. In fact, as Burnyeat goes on to say, 'The discussion in Parts II and III makes no pretence to exemplify Socrates' art of midwifery.'[3]

Let's focus especially on part II of the *Theaetetus*. Almost at the very beginning of that part, Socrates introduces a perplexity:

SOCRATES: I have something on my mind which has often bothered me before, and got me into great perplexity (*aporia*), both in my own thought and in discussion with other people—I mean, I can't say what it is, this experience we have, and how it arises in us.
THEAETETUS: What experience?
SOCRATES: Believing what is false.

(187d, Levett trans., slightly altered)

What makes Socrates' perplexity relevant to the discussion in the *Theaetetus* is that Theaetetus has just made the suggestion that perhaps knowledge is true belief. But, of course, *true* belief is a most unpromising candidate for helping us understand what knowledge is if we don't understand what *false* belief is. As Socrates develops a whole series of ingenious and memorable analyses and models of

---

[2] As Tony Long writes, 'A different kind of philosopher, the Eleatic Stranger, is needed to guide Theaetetus from the recognition of his ignorance, induced in him by Socrates, to reflections which can constitute a genuine understanding of knowledge' (Long (1998), 131). Although Long does not play up the career of perplexity in Plato the way I have in this book, his richly sensitive account of why Plato has Socrates step aside in the *Sophist* complements quite well, I think, my own suggestion.

[3] M. F. Burnyeat, 'Socratic Midwifery, Platonic Inspiration', in Benson (1992), 55.

false judgement, it becomes clear to readers how difficult it is going to be to understand how we can have false beliefs.[4]

Yet the appeal to true belief as an analysis of knowledge seems somewhat disingenuous here. After all, Plato had already had Socrates reject the suggestion that knowledge might be true belief in this memorable passage from the dialogue *Meno*:

SOCRATES: So true belief is no less useful than knowledge?

MENO: Yes, to this extent, Socrates. But the man who has knowledge will always succeed, whereas he who has true belief will only succeed at times.

SOCRATES: How do you mean? Will he who has the right belief not always succeed, as long as his belief is right?

MENO: That appears to be so of necessity, and it makes me wonder, Socrates, this being the case, why knowledge is prized far more highly than right belief, and why they are different. . . .

SOCRATES: . . . true beliefs, as long as they stay put, are a fine thing and all they do is good, but they are not willing to remain long, and they escape from a man's mind, so that they are not worth much until one ties them down with an account (*logos*) of the reason why. And that, Meno, my friend, is recollection, as we previously agreed. After they are tied down, in the first place they become knowledge, and then they remain in place. That is why knowledge is prized higher than correct opinion, and knowledge differs from correct belief in being tied down.

(97c–98a, Grube trans.)

Why didn't Plato, in the *Theaetetus*, just skip over the suggestion that knowledge is true belief and immediately take up 'true belief with an account, or justification', as the candidate for an analysis of what knowledge is? Alternatively he could have simply reminded readers of the objection from the *Meno* and gone on to criticize the third proposal, the suggestion that knowledge is true belief with an account. The criticism of the 'account' proposal clearly does break new ground in Plato's ongoing effort to say what knowledge is, whereas reconsidering the suggestion that knowledge is merely true belief seems to be a step backward.

---

[4] Here I am in agreement with McDowell (1973), 194. See also Lewis (1973) and White (1976). For more imaginative suggestions as to why Plato discusses the puzzle of false belief here see Fine (1979) and Benson (1992).

It's overwhelmingly natural to suppose that Plato had been himself perplexed about how anyone can believe anything false. How could Socrates, or anyone else who knows them both, think that Theodorus is Theaetetus? The thought is deeply puzzling. Perhaps Plato just saw here, in the context of a discussion of what knowledge is, a chance to bring out what is so maddeningly baffling about the phenomenon of false belief. So he had Theaetetus introduce the already discredited suggestion that knowledge is merely true belief so that he would have an excuse to explore the *aporia* of having a false belief.

Like many other perplexities in philosophy, this *aporia*, which occupies Socrates for almost the whole of part II of the *Theaetetus*, can be put in a question of the form 'How is it possible that *p*?'— 'How is it possible that we have false beliefs?' This is hardly the first time in the Platonic dialogues that Socrates had raised a perplexing question of the form 'How is it possible that *p*?' The Paradox of Inquiry, which we discussed in Chapter 6, easily goes into the question, 'How is it possible that I seek to find out what, for example, virtue is?' In a famous passage in the dialogue *Protagoras* Socrates ask how it is possible that one recognizes evil actions as evil and yet commits them (355a). This is the question of *akrasia*, or weakness of will.

The *Theaetetus* discussion of 'How is it possible that *p*?' differs, however, from those other discussions in several important respects. In the *Protagoras* passage Socrates argues that, in fact, it is *not* possible to perform what one recognizes to be an evil action; thus the existence of real *akrasia* is simply ruled out. In the *Theaetetus* discussion, by contrast, Socrates assumes that it *is* possible that *p*—that is, it is possible to have a false belief. In fact, we have lots of them. The puzzle is, how can it be that we have any of the genuinely false beliefs that, in fact, we have?

As for the Paradox of Inquiry, Socrates' discussion of it certainly assumes that inquiry is possible. In that respect the discussion of the Paradox of Inquiry is like Socrates' discussion of false belief. But there is an important difference. Socrates does not, in the *Meno*, accord the Paradox of Inquiry the status of a genuine perplexity. Instead, he calls it a 'contentious argument' (*eristikon logon*). Lest we not accept that dismissal, he then, as we saw in Chapter 6, brings in the Theory of Recollection and the hypothesis that all nature is akin to defuse the argument. He also offers pragmatic reasons for not allowing ourselves to be seduced by it. 'We will be better, braver and less idle,' Socrates admonishes Meno, 'if we believe that one must search for the things one does not know, rather than if we believe that it is not possible to find out what we do not know and that we must not look for it' (*Meno* 86bc).

By contrast, Socrates in the *Theaetetus* accords the puzzle about false belief full status as a genuine perplexity. His own perplexity is, indeed, what motivates the discussion. Although he is not able, in the *Theaetetus* anyway, to come up with a fully satisfactory account of how it is possible to have false beliefs, he does bring his full philosophical imagination to bear on this problem. He seems to solve it for a limited range of cases—in particular, for cases of perceptual misidentification. Thus he suggests that, knowing both Theaetetus and Theodorus, and having a memory impression of each that is like the imprint of a signet ring on a wax tablet, he might mistake each for the other by misaligning the figures approaching him with their respective memory images. Such mismatching, he suggests, is like 'people putting their shoes on the wrong feet' (*Theaetetus* 193c). In this way he might make the mistaken judgement, Theaetetus is on the right and Theodorus on the left.

Socrates ends up rejecting the wax-tablet analogy and the model of what it is to have a false belief that it suggests. But the reason is not that it fails to help us understand how perceptual misidentification might take place; the reason is that it gives us no help in understanding how mistaken belief is possible when the subject matter of the belief is non-perceptual and therefore no memory impressions come into play. His example is the mistaken belief that $7 + 5 = 11$. The solution is thus insufficiently general. But Socrates makes clear that he would like to be able to provide a general solution. With regard to this puzzle about false belief there is no speech reminiscent of the *Meno* about how we will be braver and less idle if we go on believing that there is such a thing as false belief. The puzzle is simply taken up and discussed in a businesslike way as something we ought to be able to solve.

What now about the *Sophist*? On the face of it, the *Sophist* is another 'What is F?' dialogue—where the 'F' this time is 'a sophist'. But, since a sophist is taken to be, by definition, a dissembler and charlatan, defining 'a sophist' turns out to be a way of discussing truth and falsity, as well as being and non-being. Indeed, since a necessary condition for philosophical success in defining 'a sophist' is the resolution of a family of perplexities concerning being and non-being, truth and falsity, the discussion could also, equally, perhaps even more appropriately, be said to be aimed at this goal.

Looking back at the *Theaetetus* we can say that part II of that dialogue, the part we have just been discussing on how it is possible to believe something false, is a foreshadowing of the *Sophist*. Broadened into a family of distinct, but related, perplexities—not just the one about false belief, but one about false statement, and even one about non-being—the target of *Theaetetus*, part II, could be said to be the subject under discussion in the *Sophist*.

Yet there are also important discontinuities between the *Theaetetus* and the *Sophist*. We have already discussed the intriguing fact that Socrates steps aside in the *Sophist* to let the Eleatic Stranger take over. The Stranger, as we soon see, conducts the discussion in a very different fashion from that of Socrates, the midwife. He does not induce perplexities in Theaetetus, as Socrates had, to get him to give birth to a philosophical theory or definitional analysis. Nor does anyone else induce perplexities in him. Rather, the Eleatic Stranger leads a discussion in which he himself first develops a series of perplexities and then introduces a rather daunting variety of theories and distinctions that, as he hopes to show, will resolve the perplexities. In this demonstration the Eleatic Stranger gives us a model for doing philosophy that shows as much respect for perplexity as the midwife model did. But this model, unlike that of the midwife, allows full scope for philosophical theorizing and analysis by the very person who begins by outlining the perplexities.

In the *Sophist*, we could say, perplexities themselves become a target of the inquiry. 'Really, my young friend,' the Eleatic Stranger says to Theaetetus,

this is a very difficult investigation we're engaged in. This appearing, and this seeming but not being, and this saying things but not true things—all these issues are full of perplexity (*aporias*) just as they always have been. It's extremely hard, Theaetetus, to say what form of speech we should use to say that there really is such a thing as false statement, or false belief, and moreover to say this without being caught in antinomy (*enantiologia*). (Sophist 236de, White trans., modified)

At least three different puzzles, or perplexities, are alluded to in this paragraph. There is, apparently, a puzzle about seeming but not being, one about false statement, and one about false beliefs.

The Eleatic Stranger seems to take the puzzle about false statement to be basic. The idea appears to be that, if we can be clear about what it is to make a false statement, then, since thinking is inner speech (*Sophist* 263e; cf. *Theaetetus* 189e), we should be able to handle the puzzle about false belief. Moreover, the Parmenidean warning against non-being seems to be a warning against *thinking*, falsely, that what is not, is (*Sophist* 237a). So, again, if thinking is inner speech, the underlying problem has to do with how it is we can make false statements.

Exactly what is the antinomy the Eleatic Stranger warns Theaetetus they might be caught in? It must be a puzzle about false statements. But what puzzle?

Initially at least (237a), the puzzle seems to be one that Plato had first introduced in his dialogue *Euthydemus*, at 284bc.[5] It depends on understanding what it is to make a false statement as 'not saying things that are' and taking that to mean 'saying things that are not'. Admittedly, the expression, 'saying things that are not', doesn't seem to make a great deal of sense. In so far as it makes any sense to us at all, we are doubtless inclined to gloss it as 'saying things that are not the case'. But it is important to the puzzle Plato wants to confront us with that we understand 'things that are not' to mean 'things that don't exist' so that the puzzle is this: someone who speaks falsely would have to say what is not, that is, say nothing, that is, not speak at all; thus there can be no such thing as speaking falsely (*Euthydemus* 284c).

In the dialogue *Cratylus* the *Euthydemus* puzzle reappears:

SOCRATES: Is it even possible to say that he *is* Hermogenes, if he isn't?
CRATYLUS: What do you mean?

---

[5] See Wiggins (1970).

SOCRATES: That false speaking is in every way impossible, for isn't that what *you* are trying to say? . . .

CRATYLUS: But, Socrates, how can anyone say what he says and not say something that is? And wouldn't speaking falsehoods be saying things that are not? . . .

SOCRATES: . . . Suppose you were in a foreign country and someone meeting you took your hand and said, 'Greetings! Hermogenes, son of Smicrion, visitor from Athens', would he be speaking, saying, announcing, or addressing these words not to you but to Hermogenes—or to no one? . . .

CRATYLUS: For my part, I'd say he's just making a noise and acting pointlessly, as if he were banging a brass pot.

(429d–430a, Reeve trans., modified)

Again, the crucial underlying assumption seems to be that when we speak falsely, even, as in the case above, by simply misidentifying the person we are speaking to, we say 'things that are not', that is, things that don't exist, and therefore actually say nothing. In the *Sophist*, the Eleatic Stranger moves in a related way from 'saying things, but not true things' (236e) to the implication that non-being is (237a).[6] Again there seems to be the threat that saying things that are false would have to be failing to speak.

Readers of these dialogues today are unlikely to find this puzzle about false statement, formulated in this way, very puzzling. But before we turn aside, shaking our heads, I should like to add that one can easily come up with close relatives of the simple puzzle that may give us more pause for reflection. Instead of saying that making a false statement is saying what is not, we might say instead that to make a false statement is to assert of a non-existent state of affairs that it exists. Now the perplexity-inducing question might be 'How can one pick out some particular non-existent state of affairs to say of *it* that *it* exists, when *it* doesn't—when, that is, there really is no such state of affairs to pick out?' Thus suppose I say 'Homer wrote the *Iliad*', when, in fact, no single person wrote the *Iliad*, but it was composed orally by the combined efforts of many Greek bards. How do the words of my false statement manage to pick out a determinate state of affairs, Homer writing the *Iliad*, if, in fact there has never

---

[6] See Owen (1970).

been any such state of affairs to pick out? Or, to use an example from the *Sophist*, how can one use 'Theaetetus flies' to make a false statement? To use it to make a statement at all one must be able to use it, it seems, to pick out a state of affairs. But if the statement is to be false there must be no such state of affairs for it to pick out. Wittgenstein presents a related puzzle in his *Blue Book*. 'How can one think what is not the case?' he asks, and goes on:

If I think that King's College is on fire when it is not on fire, the fact of its being on fire does not exist. Then how can I think of it?[7]

The Eleatic Stranger rejects the perplexity-inducing suggestion that in saying 'Theaetetus flies' one is simply saying 'what is not'. He would also have rejected the suggestion that one is picking out a non-existent state of affairs—that of Theaetetus flying—and saying of it that it does not exist. His proposal is rather that in saying 'Theaetetus flies' one is saying *flying* of Theaetetus when flying is different from the 'things that are concerning him', that is, different from each of the things that hold of him (263b).

To bring the discussion to a point at which this proposal can even be understood the Eleatic Stranger has had to tackle a number of important and difficult issues. Thus, for example, he points out that stringing together several verbs, or several nouns, will not yield a statement, that is, something that is a candidate for being true or false. Thus 'walks, runs, sleeps' says nothing either true or false. Nor does 'lion, stag, horse' (262a–c). The simplest sentence we can use to make a statement with a truth value will consist of a noun and a verb, as in 'Theaetetus sits', which is true, and 'Theaetetus flies', which is false (263a).

---

[7] Ludwig Wittgenstein, *The Blue and Brown Books* (New York: Harper and Row, 1960), 31. John McDowell, in McDowell (1982), quotes this passage from Wittgenstein to bring out the difference between state-of-affairs puzzles about thinking or saying something false and the related puzzles that occupy the Eleatic Stranger. For my purposes here it is enough to point out that all these puzzles are closely related.

It is interesting to note that the passage in Wittgenstein continues in a way that connects the puzzle about thinking something false to the Paradox of Inquiry: ' "How can we hang a thief who doesn't exist?" Our answer could be put in this form: "I can't hang him when he doesn't exist; but I can look for him when he doesn't exist" ' (ibid.).

Coming to understand how there can be such things as false statements thus presupposes understanding how there can be such things
as statements—bearers of truth values. It also includes understanding what it is for some of these bearers of truth values to have the
value 'true', as well as understanding what it is for some of them to
have the value 'false'. It includes not only understanding something
about being, but also something about non-being, where one form
of non-being is *being different from the things that are concerning
Theaetetus* (i.e. that hold of him).

I say that in the *Sophist* it is perplexities that are the target of the
investigation. But putting the point this way may be somewhat mis-
leading. The aim of the Eleatic Stranger in this dialogue is not simply
to target the perplexities for elimination, as a gunnery officer might
target an enemy storage depot to demolish it. The aim of the Stranger
is to use the perplexities to identify what needs to be understood and
to make resolution of perplexity a measure of success in achieving
that required understanding. Michael Frede puts the point this way:

> So the idea is not just that, by resolving the *aporia*, we can return to continue
> to claim that there are falsehoods. The idea is rather that the *aporia* helps us
> to get clearer about the precise sense in which it is true that there are false-
> hoods. It is, in part, due to an inadequate understanding of what it is for
> there to be falsehoods that we get into the *aporia*. And thus the *aporia* can be
> used constructively to get clearer about the sense in which there are false-
> hoods. Once this is clarified, the claim, made in the right sense, that there are
> falsehoods, is not only no longer threatened by the *aporia*, but also gains
> some kind of confirmation from the very fact that, taken in this sense, it no
> longer gives rise to an *aporia*.[8]

In coming to deal with this *aporia* about false statements we are
taking essential steps toward understanding what falsehood is, and
what not-being is. But, beyond that, we are also coming to understand what truth is, and what being is. In fact, it is part of the Eleatic
Stranger's purpose to show that we wouldn't be perplexed about
false statements if we were clear about the nature of true statements;
nor would we be perplexed about non-being if we were clear about
being. 'That which is and that which is not', he tells us at 250e,

---

[8] 'The Literary Form of the *Sophist*', in Gill (1996), 144.

are equally involved in perplexity (*aporias*). That is, in so far as one of them is clarified, either brightly or dimly, the other will be too.

It was thus wrong, although quite natural, to think, as is suggested in part II of the *Theaetetus*, that our perplexity about false belief is confined to the *falsity* of false belief. In fact it seeps over to the truth of true belief, just as the truth of true statements shares in the perplexity we first attributed only to the falsity of false beliefs.

What we see in the *Sophist*, then, is the development of a philosophical methodology that identifies *aporiai*, not just as obstacles to understanding the matter under investigation, but as themselves part of what needs to be investigated. This new appreciation of perplexities as targets of inquiry is developed further by Aristotle,[9] as we shall see in the next chapter.

---

[9] Michael Frede makes a similar point. Plato's procedure in the *Sophist*, he writes, 'reminds one very much of Aristotle . . . Aristotle's view is that, in order to get clear on a subject, one has, first of all, to consider in detail the *aporiai* which it raises; one's resolution of these *aporiai* will make it easy for one to say what ought to be said on the subject, and will lend support to it' (ibid. 145).

11

Perplexity and Methodology in Aristotle

In Chapter 2 we saw that Aristotle thinks philosophy begins in perplexity. More particularly, he thinks it begins in the astonished recognition that there is some basic perplexity we don't know how to deal with. He seems to have thought that the perplexities that set off the first philosophers, that is, the first Western philosophers, were puzzles about the universe. What about perplexity in Aristotle's own philosophy? What role does it play there? Does it play any continuing role at all?

Aristotle certainly uses the Greek word *aporia* commonly enough in his writings; in fact, *aporia* and its cognates turn up in almost all of his books and treatises. Unlike Plato in his early dialogues, however, Aristotle tends to use *aporia* for the puzzles or difficulties that might lead one to a state of perplexity, rather than for the state itself. Moreover, he uses it even for puzzles or difficulties that may only intrigue us, or give us second thoughts, rather than reserving it for those that bring us to a benumbed state of mental collapse.

In an interesting passage in his *De caelo* Aristotle remarks, without any suggestion that bewilderment need be involved, that 'the proofs of a theory are *aporiai* for the contrary theory' ($279^b6–7$). It is especially in passages like this one that 'difficulty' seems a better translation for *aporia* than 'perplexity', which is what seems to be called for in the Platonic dialogues.

So, even though there is plenty of talk of *aporia* in Aristotle, certainly not all that talk reports anything we might feel comfortable about calling 'Socratic perplexity'. Whether *any* of it does is a question I want now to try to answer.

As we noted in Chapter 6, Meno's eloquent avowal of philosophical perplexity at *Meno* at 80ab—what I called the 'canonical expression of Socratic perplexity'—is almost immediately followed at 80de with the Paradox of Inquiry. We find a very interesting passage in Aristotle—it occurs near the beginning of book 3 of Aristotle's *Metaphysics*—that also seems to connect *aporia* with the Paradox of Inquiry. 'We must, with a view to the science we are seeking,' Aristotle writes there,

> first recount the things that must be puzzled over (*peri ōn aporēsai dei*). These include both the other opinions that some have held on certain points, and any points besides these that happen to have been overlooked. For those who wish to get clear of perplexity (*euporēsai*) it is advantageous to state the perplexities well (*diaporēsai kalōs*); for the subsequent freedom from perplexity (*euporia*) implies the solution of the previous perplexities (*lusis tōn proteron aporoumenōn*), and it is not possible to loose a fetter one is not even aware of. But the perplexity in our thinking (*hē tēs dianoias aporia*) reveals a fetter concerning the thing [under investigation]; for in so far as our thought is in perplexity (*hē gar aporei*) it resembles people who are tied up; in both cases it is impossible to go forward. Therefore one should have surveyed all the perplexities (*diaporēsai*), both for the reasons we have stated and because people who inquire without first stating the perplexities are like those who do not know where they have to go; besides, one does not otherwise know even whether one has found what one is looking for, for the goal (*telos*) is not clear to such a person, whereas to one who has first discussed the perplexities it is clear. (995ᵃ27-ᵇ2, my trans.)

Although this is not Aristotle's only response to the Paradox of Inquiry,[1] it may be his most interesting one. Our inquiry might be thought to be a sham, Aristotle seems to be suggesting here, in an echo of the *Meno*, because we are 'like those who do not know where they have to go' and who therefore won't 'know whether [they have] found what [they are] looking for'. These two threats to the genuineness of our inquiry match exactly the two difficulties Meno had raised in first formulating the Paradox of Inquiry:

> How will you aim to search for something you do not know at all? If you should meet with it, how will you know that this is the thing that you did not know? (*Meno* 80d)

---

[1] In book 1, ch. 1 of his *Posterior Analytics*, Aristotle speaks of the Paradox as an *aporēma* and suggests that it might be resolved by distinguishing two ways of understanding 'know' in, for example, such a construction as 'know what virtue is' (71ᵃ25–30) See Ferejohn (1988).

Not only does Aristotle in this passage link *aporia* and the Paradox of Inquiry, the solution he seems to offer to the paradox focuses on *aporia*. That solution requires that the investigator aim the investigation at resolving the relevant *aporiai*. Let's pause for a moment to get clear on what this solution actually amounts to.

Consider Meno and Socrates again. They are trying to figure out what virtue is. Yet, in a way, they both already know perfectly well what virtue is. They are, after all, both competent speakers of Greek. The Greek word for virtue, *aretē*, is not a technical term, but rather a term in quite ordinary usage. Beyond that, Meno has been taken to have a special skill in discoursing on virtue. As he himself remarks, he has made many, as he had thought, very good speeches about virtue 'before large audiences on a thousand occasions'. So what's the trouble?

The trouble is that Meno cannot offer a satisfactory definitional analysis of virtue. He cannot deal with a perplexity-inducing line of reasoning that Socrates has just developed to derail Meno's attempt at definition, a line of reasoning that leads to the outrageous conclusion, 'Nobody desires bad things.' Moreover, as I tried to bring out in Chapter 5, he cannot avoid perplexity over how to understand the relation between individual virtues, such as justice and piety, and virtue as a whole. If someone could help Meno avoid the unwanted conclusion, 'Nobody desires bad things', and, at the same time, clear up the perplexity over how a single or individual virtue, such as courage, is related to the whole of virtue, Meno could, with some justification, renew his confidence that he knows perfectly well what virtue is.

Aristotle's idea of how to break this logjam is as follows. Instead of trying to aim our inquiry even more clearly at virtue, the very thing we are unclear about, and so cannot focus our sights on, we should instead focus on the perplexity or perplexities that stand in the way of our being able to call on our pre-analytic understanding of what virtue is. If we can either show what is wrong with Socrates' perplexity-inducing reasoning, or explain why it does not, after all, undermine Meno's attempt at definition, then we will have gained justified confidence that we know what virtue is.

When we see Aristotle in action, investigating what something is by focusing on the associated perplexities, we also find him appealing to our pre-analytic understanding of the thing in question. Typically he begins a philosophical investigation by stating what he takes to be the accepted truths about whatever it is he is investigating. Thus when, for example, in the first chapter of book 4 of the *Physics* he asks what *topos* (place or location) is, he mentions these five, as he supposes, uncontroversial assumptions about *topos*:

(1) The place of a thing contains it but is not part of it.
(2) A thing is neither larger nor smaller than its primary place.
(3) If something moves, it leaves its former place behind.
(4) Place always has an up and a down.
(5) Bodies have natural resting places.

Many of us today might reject (4). And most of us would find (5) puzzling or objectionable. Perhaps our list of basic assumptions would be different in other respects as well. But the important thing is that without some assumptions or other as to what place is, neither Aristotle nor we could get started trying to resolve the *aporiai* the notion of place presents.

Among the half-dozen or so *aporiai* Aristotle goes on to connect with the idea of a place, or location, are these two:

(*a*) If a body has a place, then so does its surface. But a surface doesn't really have a place, since there could be no more distinction between a surface and its place than there is between a point and its place (209ᵃ7–13).
(*b*) If every thing (in the physical world) has a place, then not only will a body have its place, but so will that place have its place. Now there will be an infinite regress of places, which is absurd (209ᵃ24–5).

We can easily imagine Aristotle's discussion of place being set in the form of an early Platonic dialogue. Thus Aristotle meets some luckless interlocutor, Orthagoras, who has lost his car keys and is trying to remember the place where he left them.

'If you are honestly trying to remember the place where you left them,' says Aristotle eagerly, 'then you must certainly know what a place is. Please enlighten me.'

The discussion then proceeds in the usual way. First, Orthagoras gives Aristotle mere examples of places where he might have left his car keys (the hall table, the dresser drawer, his right jacket pocket, etc.), to which Aristotle would reply that he is not interested in examples; he wants to know the *idea* or *eidos* that these various places have in common, that is, what makes them all places.

When Orthagoras finally does produce a candidate definition, Aristotle responds, 'What then about places themselves, my dear Orthagoras? If a body has a place, surely its surface also has a place' (etc.). Or: 'What then about places themselves, my friend Orthagoras? If everything in the physical world has a place, then surely a place, if it is not a mere nothing, also has a place. But then its place would also have a place and there would be an infinite regress of places, which is absurd.'

Would our imagined dialogue also include a profession of Socratic-style ignorance, in this case, Aristotelian ignorance? Would Aristotle say, 'I don't know any more than you do, my dear Orthagoras, what place is'? The *Physics* passage certainly contains no such profession of ignorance. It may be, of course, that Aristotle was himself once baffled and bewildered about place. Indeed, he may have been once benumbed and in the grip of *aporia* (*a*), or *aporia* (*b*), or both (*a*) and (*b*). But Aristotle, as the author of the *Physics*, gives no evidence of being plagued by any persisting bafflement about place.

Of course, we, as readers, may find Aristotle's solution to the *aporiai* he lists less than fully satisfying. To (*a*) Aristotle responds by saying that neither surfaces nor lines have places. We may find that response ad hoc and unmotivated. To (*b*) Aristotle says that, even though a place may be said to be in a place, it is in a place only in a different sense of 'in' from that in which a body may be said to be in a place, and so there is no infinite regress. As readers, we may be dissatisfied with Aristotle's resolutions of these two perplexities. Still, whether or not one finds Aristotle's resolutions of the perplexities he lists satisfactory, the idea that resolving those perplexities would show one's analysis to be on target seems a good one.

Aristotle's discussion of time, five chapters later in the *Physics*, follows the same methodology, but with quite a different result! On the surface, the discussion of time is just as orderly and well-controlled as the discussion of place. But closer inspection reveals a surprising number of loose ends.

Aristotle begins the discussion of time with three *aporiai*, which he introduces with the dark remark that they might make one suspect that time 'either does not exist at all, or just barely and indistinctly' (217^b32-3). (There had been no similar suggestion that perhaps place does not exist at all, or perhaps only barely and indistinctly.) Aristotle continues:

> (1) Some of it has been and is not, some of it is to be and is not yet. From these both [that is, from what no longer is and what is not yet] infinite time and any arbitrary time are composed. But it would seem to be impossible that what is composed of things that are not should participate in being. ($217^b33-218^a3$)
>
> (2) Further, it is necessary that, of everything that is resoluble into parts, if it is, either all the parts or some of them should be when it is. But of time, while it is resoluble into parts, if it is, either all the parts or some of them should be when it is. But of time, while it is resoluble into parts, some [parts] have been, some are to be, and none is. The now is not a part, for a part measures [the whole], and the whole must be composed of the parts, but time is not thought to be composed of nows. (218^a3-8)
>
> (3) Again, it is not easy to see whether the now, which appears to be the boundary between past and future, remains always one and the same or is different from time to time. (218^a8-11, Hussey trans.)

Aristotle then goes on to elaborate on the last of these three perplexities, before he takes up the contending theories about what time is. As part of his own account of what time is, Aristotle also seeks to resolve that third *aporia*. Thus, after going to great lengths to make it seem utterly inconceivable that the now can always remain one and the same and, then, similarly inconceivable that the now could be different from time to time, Aristotle tries to give us this assurance: 'The now is in a way the same, and in a way not the same: considered as being at different stages, it is different—that is what it is for it to be a now—but whatever it is that makes it a now is the same' (219^b12-15, Hussey trans.).

No doubt some of Aristotle's readers are not reassured by this solution. But much more striking than the shortcomings of Aristotle's solution to this *aporia* is the utter absence of *any* attempt whatsoever to resolve the first two *aporiai*. Although later commentators have busied themselves with inventive and resourceful suggestions as to how Aristotle *should* have resolved them, I think it is fair to say that no satisfactory resolutions present themselves in Aristotle's *Physics*, or anywhere else in Aristotle's writings, for that matter.

There are other loose ends in Aristotle's discussion of time. Thus, for example, having concluded that 'time is the number of motion in respect of before and after' (220ᵃ35), Aristotle adds that time will also measure what is at rest. But how can it be a measure of rest, if it is, by definition, the number of *motion* with respect to before and after? Aristotle never explains. He does assert, 'Since time is the measure of motion, it will be the measure of rest, too' (221ᵇ7–8). Yet, uncharacteristically, he gives no reasoning to back up that crucial claim. Even if, in and of itself, the claim seems perfectly reasonable, when we keep in mind that it is by definition that time is the measure of *motion*, and certainly not by definition that it is the measure of rest, we may easily become perplexed about why it should follow, either from the definition itself, or from the definition plus some obvious truth, that time is also the measure of rest.

Aristotle never owns up to the full force of perplexities about time that seem to afflict him. An impartial observer, I suggest, might well conclude not only that his discussion of time could provide wonderful material for a Socratic-style dialogue on what time is, but also that such a dialogue ought to be an *aporetic* dialogue.

A surprising expression of truly Socratic perplexity turns up in book 2 of Aristotle's *Generation of Animals*. The problem Aristotle sets himself in chapter 10 of that book is to understand the nature of honey bees. 'There is much perplexity (*pollēn aporian*)', Aristotle admits at the beginning of the chapter, 'about the generation of bees' (759ᵃ8). As he goes on to make clear, he simply doesn't understand at all how honey bees reproduce. For one thing he doesn't understand the role the queen bee (called by him, and other ancients, 'the king'—basileus) plays in reproduction. For another, he can't identify the gender of either the workers or the drones. He thinks it unreasonable to suppose that the worker bees are female and the drones male, since, as he puts it, nature does not give weapons for fighting to any female, and, while the drones are stingless, all the bees have a sting. Nor is the opposite view reasonable, that the [worker] bees are male and the drones female, for no males are in the habit of working for their offspring, but as it is, the [worker] bees do this. (759^{b}1–6, Platt trans.)

Aristotle is so flummoxed by bees that he realizes his theory may be distorting the facts that the theory is actually supposed to explain. 'The facts', he admits, uncharacteristically, 'have not been sufficiently grasped; if ever they are,' he continues, 'then credit must be given rather to observation than to theories, and to the theories only if what they affirm agrees with the observed facts' (760^{a}29–34). Here is something strikingly like Socratic ignorance, though limited specifically to honey bees!

So far we have noted three roles that perplexity plays in the philosophy of Aristotle. First, it plays an essential role in Aristotle's account of the origin of philosophy. Astonishment that one cannot resolve basic perplexities, he says, leads people to philosophize. Second, perplexity plays a crucial role in Aristotle's own philosophical methodology. Partly, no doubt, in response to the Paradox of Inquiry, Aristotle suggests that we focus our philosophical investigation on its target by first collecting the received opinions on the matter to be investigated and by then assembling the perplexities that plague this topic. The investigation will be a success, he suggests, if our theory or analysis respects most of the received opinions, or at least the most reputable of them, and also resolves the perplexities.

Third, a numbing Socratic perplexity sometimes resists Aristotle's best efforts to resolve the difficulties he has identified. We found evidence of such perplexity in Aristotle's discussion of time and also in his failure to understand the honey bee.

There is one further development concerning *aporia* in Aristotle that I want to highlight. Sometimes Aristotle figures out a way to extricate himself from what seem to him clearly unresolvable perplexities. The best example of this that I am aware of concerns the question, 'How do I know whether I am now dreaming?' We moderns associate this question with Descartes. But, as I already pointed out in Chapter 1, the question is to be found in Plato's *Theaetetus* at 158bc. Plato seems not to know what to do with it. He has Socrates abandon it to discuss other matters. What Aristotle does is to reject its claim to be a genuine *aporia*. Here is the passage:

> Some . . . are perplexed (*aporousi*) because they want to know who will judge who is healthy, and in general on each subject [who is to say] who will judge it correctly. Such perplexities (*aporēmata*) are similar to the perplexing question (*tō aporein*) 'Are we now asleep or awake?' and they all have the same force. For those who pose them ask for an argument for everything; for they seek a principle, and they seek to get it through demonstration . . . Their trouble is just as we have stated: for they seek an argument for something for which there is no argument, for a principle of demonstration is not a demonstration. (Metaphysics 4, 1011ᵃ3–13, Kirwan trans.)

Aristotle, in this passage, compares the philosopher who takes seriously the question, 'How do I know whether I am now dreaming?' to someone who wants a demonstration for a principle of demonstration. If, as Lewis Carroll brings out in 'What the Tortoise said to Achilles',[2] we add the needed rule of inference, or principle of demonstration, to an argument as an additional premiss, we invite someone to point out that we now need a new rule of inference to connect the original premisses with the rule of inference to get the conclusion. If we make the further rule of inference a yet additional premiss, we are on the road to an infinite regress.

Thus suppose we have a simple *modus ponens* argument:

(1) P
(2) If P then Q.

Therefore

(3) Q.

The validity of this inference, one might complain, depends upon the *rule* of *modus ponens*, which we could formulate as

(4) Whenever we have some premiss, A, and another premiss, if A then B, then we may conclude B.

But if we add this rule of inference, as a premiss, to the argument, we open ourselves up to needing an additional premiss, such as this one:

---

[2] *Mind*, NS 4/14 (1895), 278–80.

(5) Whenever we have some premiss, A, and another premiss, if A then B, and the rule, (4), then we may conclude B.

And so on ad infinitum.

Aristotle seems to think that the philosopher who takes the dream question as a serious perplexity invites an infinite regress in a similar way. Perhaps his idea is this. Suppose I had a test for whether I am now dreaming. Call the test 'T' and the application of the test to my present experience 'T–1'. Suppose T–1 indicates that I am awake. Does that settle things? Not at all. How do I know that I was not merely dreaming that I applied T successfully on this occasion? In response to that worry I might try applying T to my first application of T, that is, to T–1. Call this application of T to T–1 'T–2'. Suppose, again, that T–2 indicates I was awake during the first application of my test, that is, during T–1. Does that settle the question? Not at all. The same question could be raised about T–2, and so on ad infinitum.

By ruling the dream question illegitimate in this way Aristotle clearly aims to keep it from benumbing us into a state of philosophical paralysis. The message is that not everything we find initially perplexing is genuinely worthy of being perplexed about. Sometimes it is only clearly mistaken assumptions that generate perplexity. In this case what seems to make the dream question legitimately perplexing is only the mistaken assumption that one could apply a dream test to one's present experience in such a way that one could be sure one wasn't only dreaming that one was applying it. Once we see that there could not be such a thing as a certifiably 'undreamable' test for determining whether one is dreaming, Aristotle reasons, one will see that the question 'How do I know whether I am now dreaming?' does not express a *legitimate* perplexity.

Here, then, are some of the ways that Aristotle normalizes perplexity in the practice of philosophy. He makes collecting perplexities an important step in organizing and directing an inquiry. He broadens the scope of perplexity so as to include, not only ethical perplexities, such as the ones Socrates had first called attention to, and even the metaphysical and epistemological perplexities Plato had added to the list, but also puzzles in such sciences as cosmology and biology. Finally, he brands some perplexities, for example, the notorious one about how I can know whether I am now dreaming, as illegitimate, or spurious.

From an Aristotelian perspective it is an irony of modern philosophy that so much of it turns on the assumption that the question about whether one is now dreaming, and the related question about whether *all* this life might be one's own dream, are legitimate perplexities. Poor Aristotle! Poor us! If we today, at the end of the twentieth century, have left dream scepticism behind it is only to take up another perplexing possibility that Aristotle would have considered equally illegitimate: How do I know that I am not merely a brain in a vat?[3] As if one could prove everything!

---

[3] Cf. Daniel C. Dennett, 'Where Am I?', in his *Brainstorms* (Cambridge, Mass.: MIT Press, 1978), 310–23.

12

Socratic Perplexity and the Nature of Philosophy

IN the previous chapters I have made an effort to redirect the way we think about Socratic perplexity in the dialogues of Plato. I have also tried to awaken a new appreciation for the importance of perplexity to philosophy, and to enhance our understanding of the variety of ways perplexity may be used, treated, or appealed to, in doing philosophy. Let me elaborate a bit on each of those two aims. First, let's consider afresh the role of perplexity in the dialogues of Plato.

To many commentators, the aporetic dialogues of Plato are something of a problem, even an embarrassment. Why should arguably the greatest writer in our whole philosophical tradition have written works that end in failure? And how could one of the cleverest and most astute thinkers of all time not have known how to answer the apparently simple questions he has Socrates raise, especially in the early dialogues?

For those commentators who are confident they can extract the philosophy of Socrates from the early writings of Plato, the embarrassment may be especially acute. Although aporetic dialogues make up only a small proportion of the total Platonic corpus, the proportion of aporetic dialogues within the set of *early* Platonic dialogues, that is, within the set of those dialogues that can most plausibly be thought to present 'the philosophy of Socrates', is much greater. The heavy weight of failure in the seemingly most authentic Socratic dialogues may lead us ask, (1) did Socrates himself reach any positive conclusions at all by his philosophical method? And (2) if he did, how did he manage this feat, given that his 'elenctic method', so well illustrated in some of the aporetic dialogues, seems to consist only in examining for consistency the beliefs of his interlocutors?

Even commentators who give a resoundingly affirmative answer to question (1), and thus insist that Socrates reaches positive conclusions, find it difficult to deal with the aporetic dialogues. Many of them try to argue that such aporetic dialogues as the *Laches* and the *Euthyphro* really contain hints and suggestions of answers to the issues they raise. The alert reader, it is supposed, will pick up the hints and suggestions, perhaps putting together what Socrates says or hints at in one dialogue with what he says or hints at in another to yield a genuinely philosophical doctrine.

Commentators who remain sceptical about the possibility of successfully extracting 'the philosophy of Socrates' from the early dialogues of Plato are also easily caught up in the search for a 'hidden meaning' behind Plato's aporetic dialogues. They may think Plato wrote these dialogues as introductory exercises for the reader. On such an understanding of these dialogues, the reader is meant to figure out what this or that character missed, perhaps even what Socrates himself missed, or, for some reason, allowed to go unchallenged. One entirely admirable idea behind this approach is the idea that philosophy is a do-it-yourself activity.[1] Plato, it may thus be suggested, often fails to let Socrates endorse the answers that Plato thinks are correct, but, the assumption continues, we can expect him to have left his readers with enough clues to be able to figure out for themselves what the right answers are. Having to figure out the answers for ourselves, according to this way of viewing the dialogues, makes us more likely both to understand those answers and to accept them as correct.

More sweepingly, a commentator who doubts that we can extract the philosophy of Socrates from the early dialogues of Plato may view all the aporetic dialogues as groundwork needed for the acceptance of Plato's mature philosophy, as it is presented in the middle dialogues. Thus, according to Charles Kahn, the aporetic dialogue is Plato's

---

[1] Consider, for example, Charles Griswold's comment in his introduction to the collection, *Platonic Writings, Platonic Readings*: '[Diskin] Clay's reading of the *Republic* suggests that deficiencies, paradoxes, tensions, and even fallacies in a Platonic dialogue ought to be taken not as signalling Plato's inability to reason well but as intentionally designed invitations to the reader to sort through the topic at hand himself' (Griswold (1988), 5).

literary device for reinterpreting the Socratic elenchus as the preparation for constructive philosophy. The reader is to accompany the interlocutor in the recognition of a problem. But the more astute reader will also recognize some hints of a solution. Hence the tension between the *surface* [*emphasis mine*] conclusion in *aporia* and the implicit hints of positive doctrine.[2]

Commenting on the slave-boy episode in the *Meno* Kahn writes:

Meno will not learn much from this lesson. But we the readers are allowed to see that this is the function of *aporia* generally and of the aporetic dialogues in particular: to eliminate the false belief that these are simple matters, easily understood, and to instill a desire for further inquiry. Hence the aporetic dialogues are all also protreptic, urging us on to the practice of philosophy.[3]

As for (2) above, and the worry about how the cross-examination of elenchus can, by itself, lead to positive conclusions, Gregory Vlastos made it the major project of the later part of his long and productive life as a Socrates scholar to show how the elenctic method could be supplemented with assumptions that would make it yield positive results.[4] The influence of Vlastos on subsequent Socratic scholarship has been enormous. Vlastos enlisted many of our ablest and most gifted Socratic scholars in the effort to answer (2), or else show why Vlastos's own answer falls short of the mark. And much recent scholarship on the philosophy of Socrates is aimed at either supporting and amplifying Vlastos's conclusions or else at criticizing them within the context of the project he set for himself.

Let's suppose for the moment, with Vlastos, that the early dialogues of Plato do give us an at least moderately accurate picture of the historical Socrates. To me the most intriguing and significant feature of that portrait is Socratic perplexity. To Vlastos, by contrast, Socratic perplexity is of little significance. This can be established quickly and easily by checking the hundred-word Greek index to the crowning work of his scholarship on Socrates, *Socrates: Ironist and Moral Philosopher*.[5] Missing altogether from the 'Index of Greek Words' are the Greek word for perplexity, *aporia*, and its cognates.

---

[2] Kahn (1996), 100.　　[3] Ibid. 180.

[4] Perhaps Vlastos's most ambitious effort to do that is to be found in his paper 'The Socratic Elenchus', *Oxford Studies in Ancient Philosophy*, 1 (1983), 27–58.

[5] (Ithaca, NY: Cornell University Press, 1991).

Nor is there in the main text of Vlastos's book any discussion at all of Socratic perplexity. The only discussion of perplexity at all in the book appears in an appendix titled 'The *Hippias Minor*—Sophistry or Honest Perplexity'.[6]

Why does it matter? Why is it important to recognize and celebrate Socratic perplexity? Suppose that the early Platonic dialogues do give us a reasonably accurate portrayal of Plato's teacher. Why is it important that that teacher could reduce otherwise perfectly articulate interlocutors to perplexity? And why is it important that he insisted he was at least as perplexed about the matter under investigation as his interlocutor? Alternatively, suppose that the figure of Socrates in even the early dialogues is almost wholly a creation of Plato. In that case, why is it important that Plato wrote dialogues that end in perplexity? And why is it important that he gave a prominent place to perplexity, and perplexities, even in some of his middle and late dialogues, which no one thinks are accurate portraits of the historical Socrates?

One response to these questions that one can find well represented in the best recent literature on Socrates and Plato is formulated this way by Thomas Brickhouse and Nicholas Smith:

Socrates' investigations often reduce his interlocutors to *aporia* by showing that his interlocutor's responses to his questions are inconsistent. The interlocutor must recognize and resolve the inconsistencies in his beliefs, or his whole life will be in discord.[7]

In a similar vein, Terence Irwin has this to say specifically about the dialogue *Laches*:

Laches, for instance, finds that he cannot both define bravery as standing firm and admit that sometimes a tactical retreat is the brave action. He agrees that he must reject the proposed definition. After further questions, Laches finds himself agreeing that fearlessness and resolution are always brave; that bravery is a virtue; and that a virtue is always fine and beneficial; and that fearless resolution is sometimes disgraceful and harmful.[8]

As Irwin goes on to emphasize, these beliefs are, in fact, inconsistent. 'Socrates seeks to amend and improve an interlocutor's beliefs,'

---

[6] (Ithaca, NY: Cornell University Press, 1991) 275–80.
[7] Brickhouse and Smith (1994), 73.   [8] Irwin (1989), 74–5.

Irwin tells us, 'not to destroy them.'[9] One way to amend and improve Laches' beliefs, one might have thought, is, quite simply, to render them consistent. Yet such a project is surely not Socrates' sole aim, or even his primary aim, even in the early dialogues. If it were, he would be what we could appropriately call 'a client-centred cognitive therapist', rather than a true philosopher. But, clearly, he is a true philosopher. Being a true philosopher, he wants to know what bravery is, and what piety is, and what virtue is, not just what we can do to develop a consistent belief-set concerning courage, or piety, or virtue. He makes us realize that important conceptual difficulties stand in the way of this project, difficulties that induce perplexity.

As Irwin himself brings out elsewhere, Socrates' project in the early dialogues cannot be primarily one of merely helping his interlocutors to attain consistent beliefs about the virtues. Thus here is part of what Irwin says about the early dialogue *Charmides*:

The *Charmides* ends aporetically, but we should not infer that Socrates has no firm view about the character of temperance. On the contrary, it is his firm view that creates the puzzle . . . Socrates thinks *we are right to be puzzled and confused* [emphasis mine]. But he believes that common sense cannot reasonably reject his arguments.[10]

The point, then, is not that Charmides should simply alter his beliefs about temperance so as to develop a consistent set, or that we, the readers of the dialogue, should see to it that our beliefs about temperance form a consistent set. The point is rather there is something inherently perplexing about the common-sense notion of temperance. Philosophy needs to address this inherent perplexity.

Philosophy often begins in such perplexity. A beginning question in philosophy might be 'What is time?' or 'What is knowledge?' The historical Socrates may have confined himself primarily, or even exclusively, to ethical matters, as Aristotle asserts in book 1 of his *Metaphysics*, at 987^{b}1. So his questions may have been, as Plato reports in the *Meno*, 'What is virtue?' or 'What is courage?' (*Laches*) or 'What is piety?' (*Euthyphro*).

---

9 Ibid. 75.   10 Irwin (1995), 42.

One reason philosophy often begins in perplexity is that philosophy deals with inherently problematic concepts, concepts like time and justice, mind, and causality—concepts we all seem to be able to use, and so to understand, but concepts of which we also find it difficult, if not impossible, to give a satisfactory analysis.

When I say that philosophy deals with inherently problematic concepts, my claim is not based so much on a theory about the domain of philosophy as it is on a study of the history of philosophy. Concepts central to the thinking of Plato, Aristotle, Augustine, Aquinas, Descartes, Spinoza, Leibniz, Locke, Berkeley, Hume, and Kant—to mention a few of Western philosophy's luminaries—remain problematic today. We have made important advances across the centuries in the ways we use and think about these concepts. But we are not now able, nor are we likely to be able in the near future, to give accounts of these concepts that will stand unchallenged for all later time. A natural conclusion to draw is that these concepts are inherently problematic.

A philosopher who can make us appreciate how problematic a concept like knowledge or virtue or time or causality or life or mind is, does us a service, even if we are never able to come up with a satisfactory analysis of that concept, or a viable theory that explains the phenomena grouped under it. As Socrates says to Theaetetus, 'If you remain barren, you will be gentler and more agreeable to your companions, having the good sense not to fancy you know what you do not know' (*Theaetetus* 210c). This is the wisdom of Socratic ignorance.

I think here of Morton White's tribute to G. E. Moore, who is perhaps the twentieth-century philosopher most devoted to a Socratic-style definitional analysis of philosophically problematic concepts:

Because he was so cautious about saying that one expression meant the same as another, Moore seemed to be left with a set of *un*analyzable concepts in one hand, and in the other a set of concepts about whose analysis he was never certain. The result was that one of the greatest philosophical analysts of our age found it hard to point, in all honesty, to a single successful analysis of an important philosophical idea.[11]

[11] Morton White, 'Memories of G. E. Moore', *Journal of Philosophy*, 57 (1960), 808.

There is, of course, the danger that, when philosophy gives us no answers, only questions and perplexities, we will become cynical and nihilistic, not gentle and modest. This danger seems to have pre-occupied Plato while he was writing the *Republic*. It lies behind the strictures at the end of book 7 against introducing philosophy to young people. The danger of turning our young students into cynics and nihilists is one that all of us who have ever taught introductory courses in philosophy have become aware of.

In addition to the worry about making young people nihilists and cynics, there is for us teachers of philosophy a certain frustration in having always to bring up difficulties and shortcomings for each philosophical theory or analysis we discuss. Perhaps it was just such a frustration that led Plato to propose, in the *Meno*, the 'method of hypothesis' to move beyond the negative result of repeated stalemate in asking what virtue is.

Sometimes we may suspect that the grounds for our perplexity are sophistical. Socrates in the *Meno* manages to avoid being perplexed by the Paradox of Inquiry by framing two grand hypotheses in response to it. As if fearful that we may not accept his hypotheses, he goes on to admonish us that we will be better and braver if we do not allow ourselves to be taken in by the paradox. Should he have addressed the paradox more directly? Could he have done so? How can we be sure that the grounds of our perplexity are not merely sophistical?

Most of us hope, at least some of the time, that perplexity will lead directly to philosophical theory. This expectation seems to lie behind what I have called the 'instrumental' uses of perplexity in the *Phaedo* and the *Republic*. Yet there is always the fear that even our best philosophical theory, perhaps conceived in answer to perplexity, may, in turn, generate its own perplexity. That is what I called in Chapter 8 'second-order perplexity'. The perplexities Plato reveals in part I of his dialogue *Parmenides* are some of the most profound examples of second-order perplexity in all of philosophy.

So then is philosophy just an endless cycle of perplexity? Is it that one begins by becoming appropriately perplexed about something that is genuinely problematic, one moves on to a philosophical theory or a philosophical analysis that is meant to deal with the perplexity, and then one finds that the theory, or the analysis, generates its own perplexity?

What Plato does in the *Theaetetus* and *Sophist*, I have suggested, is twofold. First, he delineates a distinct role for the Socratic midwife who has forsworn all ambition to produce a philosophical theory himself. The lack of ambition to produce his own philosophical theory of knowledge, or definitional analysis of what knowledge is, gives Socrates in the *Theaetetus* a valuable objectivity and disinterestedness. He would like to attend the birth of a viable theory. But his job is to induce genuine labour pains and to allay them only where doing so is justified.

It is crucial that we appreciate the value and importance of Socratic midwifery even when all that the investigation yields is windeggs. There is great worth in having come to appreciate what is problematic about the idea of knowing something, or the idea of being pious, even if one never comes up with a satisfactory account of what knowledge or piety is.

After having secured the integrity of his midwife figure, Plato does a second thing; he introduces a philosophical role distinct from the midwife, namely that of the Eleatic Stranger. The Stranger, in the *Sophist*, is hardly insensitive to philosophical perplexity. Quite the opposite is true. But the Stranger can seek to 'normalize' perplexity by identifying, diagnosing, and perhaps resolving particular, specifiable perplexities, that is, specifiable problems, puzzles, or difficulties that naturally give rise to the state of philosophical perplexity. Already in the middle section of the *Theaetetus*, but throughout the *Sophist*, perplexities become themselves the targets of inquiry.

Aristotle, as we noted in the last chapter, makes the identification of philosophical perplexities about time, or place, or whatever the subject for investigation is, part of his response to the Paradox of Inquiry. An investigation into the nature of, say, time (or virtue, or causality) will have been shown to be targeted successfully at time, say, rather than at something that might be confused with time if, among other things, we have been able to identify the perplexities that go with thinking about time, and we have been able to resolve those perplexities satisfactorily.

Aristotle does another interesting thing with perplexity. Picking up on a subtle shift in late Plato, Aristotle applies the Greek word *aporia* not to the benumbed state of bafflement so memorable in the early Platonic dialogues, but rather to identifiable puzzles, conundrums, or difficulties that might lead us to such bafflement. Although this shift is already under way in part II of Plato's *Theaetetus* and in his *Sophist*, it is Aristotle who focuses decisively on distinct perplex-it*ies*, rather than the state of philosophical perplexity.

Aristotle also makes a principled move to cordon off perplexities deemed to be simply intractable. He argues that such perplexities can safely be ignored, if, like the question as to whether I am now dreaming, they demand of us something conceptually or pragmatically impossible. We need, of course, to be concerned that such dismissals are really justified. Here, and elsewhere in our response to Socratic perplexity, it may be helpful to have in our company a Socratic midwife to keep us honest. Many of our philosophy departments today, I suggest, exemplify this last insight by including at least one Socratic midwife on the faculty, as well as several Eleatic Strangers. (The unfairness is, quite obviously, that it is easier for the Eleatic Strangers to gain tenure in philosophy departments than it is for the Socratic midwives to do so!)

Many of us teachers of philosophy try to be Socratic midwives on at least a part-time basis, even though we cannot be satisfied with full-time barrenness. We are part-time midwives because we suspect that, unless we can induce fresh puzzlement in ourselves, as well as our students, we will not be fair to the full profundity of philosophical questions. If we develop an account of the nature of justice, or a position on whether a computer could be built that thinks, and we develop this account or position without giving it a fully perplexity-inviting examination, we feel that we have shut out Socrates and betrayed our profession.

Yet most of us are, at most, only part-time midwives. We want to be pregnant with our own babies. We want philosophical results, and we want to generate them in and from ourselves. So, like the Eleatic Stranger, and like Aristotle, we seek to turn philosophical perplexity into philosophical problems, or difficulties, that we might have some hope of solving, or resolving, if not for all time, at least for our own time.

Retelling the story of philosophical perplexity from the Presocratics through Socrates and Plato to Aristotle need not, then, be simply an exercise in intellectual history. For us full-time philosophers, anyway, it can also be an adventure in self-understanding. Regardless of how we sort out the tangled issues of how the historical Socrates is related to the figure of Socrates in the early Platonic dialogues (or, indeed, the middle and later dialogues!), the career of perplexity in the writings of Plato is something that many of us can find we have recapitulated in our own philosophical lives. And whatever our final judgement on Aristotle as an historian of philosophy might turn out to be, his comments on Presocratic philosophers, on Socrates, and on Plato, as well as his own various attitudes toward *aporia*, provide a rich and suggestive framework for assessing the roles of perplexity in philosophy today. In our own philosophical lives many of us have found that, like the fabled sculptures of Daedalus that Plato is so fond of referring to in his dialogues, philosophical perplexity refuses both to stay put and to go away.

REFERENCES

I. BOOKS

ALLEN, R. E. (1970), *Plato's 'Euthyphro' and the Earlier Theory of Forms* (London: Routledge and Kegan Paul).

BENSON, HUGH H. (1992), ed., *Essays on the Philosophy of Socrates* (Oxford: University Press).

BOSTOCK, DAVID (1986), *Plato's* Phaedo (Oxford: Clarendon Press).

—— (1988), *Plato's* Theaetetus (Oxford: Clarendon Press).

BRICKHOUSE, THOMAS C., and SMITH, NICHOLAS D. (1994), *Plato's Socrates* (Oxford University Press).

FINE, GAIL (1993), *On Ideas: Aristotle's Criticism of Plato's Theory of Forms* (Oxford: Clarendon Press).

FREDE, MICHAEL, and STRIKER, GISEAL (1996), *Rationality in Greek Thought* (Oxford: Clarendon Press).

GENTZLER, JYL (1998), ed., *Method in Ancient Philosophy* (Oxford: Clarendon Press).

GILL, CHRISTOPHER, and MCCABE, MARY MARGARET (1996), eds., *Form and Argument in Late Plato* (Oxford: Clarendon Press).

GRISWOLD, CHARLES L., Jr. (1988), *Platonic Writings, Platonic Readings* (New York: Routledge).

HARE, R. M. (1982), *Plato* (Oxford: University Press).

HYLAND, DREW A. (1995), *Finitude and Transcendence in the Platonic Dialogues* (Albany: State University of New York Press).

IRWIN, TERENCE (1989), *Classical Thought* (Oxford: Oxford University Press).

—— (1995), *Plato's Ethics* (New York: Oxford University Press).

JAEGER, WERNER (1944), *Paideia: The Ideals of Greek Culture*, vol. ii, trans. G. Highet (New York: Oxford University Press).

KAHN, CHARLES H. (1996), *Plato and the Socratic Dialogue: The Philosophical Use of a Literary Form* (Cambridge: University Press).

KRAUT, RICHARD (1992), ed., *The Cambridge Companion to Plato* (Cambridge: University Press).

MCDOWELL, JOHN (1973), *Plato:* Theatetus (Oxford: Clarendon, Press).

McPherran, Mark L. (1996), *The Religion of Socrates* (University Park, Pa.: Pennsylvania State University Press).

Mates, Benson (1996), *The Skeptic Way: Sextus Empiricus's* Outlines of Pyrrhonism (New York: Oxford University Press).

Meinwald, Constance C. (1991), *Plato's Parmenides* (New York: Oxford University Press).

Nails, Debra (1995), *Agora, Academy, and the Conduct of Philosophy* (Dordrecht: Kluwer).

Owen, G. E. L. (1986), *Logic, Science and Dialectic* (Ithaca, NY: Cornell University Press).

Ryle, Gilbert (1966), *Plato's Progress* (Cambridge: University Press).

Smith, Robin (1997), *Aristotle's* Topics: *Books I and VIII* (Oxford: Clarendon Press).

Vander Waerdt, Paul A. (1994), *The Socratic Movement* (Ithaca, NY: Cornell University Press).

Vlastos, Gregory (1970), ed., *Plato: A Collection of Critical Essays*, i: *Metaphysics and Epistemology* (Garden City, NY: Anchor Books).

—— (1971), ed., *The Philosophy of Socrates: A Collection of Critical Essays* (Garden City, NY: Anchor Books).

—— (1981), *Platonic Studies*, 2nd edn. (Princeton: University Press).

—— (1991), *Socrates: Ironist and Moral Philosopher* (Ithaca, NY: Cornell University Press).

—— (1994), *Socratic Studies* (Cambridge: University Press).

—— (1995), *Studies in Greek Philosophy*, ii: *Socrates, Plato, and their Tradition*, ed. Daniel W. Graham (Princeton: University Press).

White, Nicholas P. (1976), *Plato on Knowledge and Reality* (Indianapolis: Hackett).

II. ARTICLES

Benson, Hugh H. (1990), 'Meno, the Slave Boy and the Elenchos', *Phronesis*, 35: 128–58.

—— (1992), 'Why is there a Discussion of False Belief in the *Theaetetus*?', *Journal of the History of Philosophy*, 30: 171–99.

Bolton, Robert (1993), 'Aristotle's Account of the Socratic Elenchus', *Oxford Studies in Ancient Philosophy*, 11: 121–52.

Burnyeat, Myles F. (1977), 'Socratic Midwifery, Platonic Inspiration', *Bulletin of the Institute of Classical Studies*, 24: 7–16; repr. in Benson (1992), 53–65.

CALEF, SCOTT WARREN (1995*a*), 'Piety and the Unity of Virtue in *Euthyphro* 11E–14C', *Oxford Studies in Ancient Philosophy*, 13: 1–26.

—— (1995*b*), 'Further Reflections on Socratic Piety: A Reply to Mark McPherran', *Oxford Studies in Ancient Philosophy*, 13: 37–43.

CHARLTON, WILLIAM (1995), 'Plato's Later Platonism', *Oxford Studies in Ancient Philosophy*, 13: 113–33.

COHEN, S. MARC (1971*a*), 'Socrates on the Definition of Piety: *Euthyphro* 10A–11B', *Journal of the History of Philosophy*, 9: 1–13; repr. in Vlastos (1971), 158–76.

—— (1971*b*), 'The Logic of the Third Man', *Philosophical Review*, 80: 448–75.

FEREJOHN, MICHAEL (1988), 'Meno's Paradox and *De Re* Knowledge in Aristotle's Theory of Demonstration', *History of Philosophy Quarterly*, 5: 99–117.

FINE, GAIL (1979), 'False Belief in the *Theaetetus*', *Phronesis*, 24: 70–80.

FREDE, MICHAEL (1992), 'Plato's Arguments and the Dialogue Form', *Oxford Studies in Ancient Philosophy*, suppl. vol., *Methods of Interpreting Plato and his Dialogues* (Oxford: Clarendon Press), 201–19.

—— (1996), 'The Literary Form of the *Sophist*', in Gill (1996), 135–51.

GEACH, P. T. (1966), 'Plato's *Euthyphro*; An Analysis and Commentary', *Monist*, 50: 369–82; repr. in P. T. Geach, *Logic Matters* (Oxford: Blackwell, 1972), 31–44.

GRAHAM, DANIEL W. (1992), 'Socrates and Plato', *Phronesis*, 37: 141–65.

KAHN, CHARLES H. (1981), 'Did Plato Write Socratic Dialogues?', *Classical Quarterly*, 31: 305–20; repr. in Benson (1992), 35–52.

LEWIS, FRANK A. (1973), 'Two Paradoxes in the *Theaetetus*', in J. M. E. Moravcsik (ed.), *Patterns in Plato's Thought* (Dordrecht: Reidel), 123–49.

LONG, A. A. (1998), 'Plato's Apologies and Socrates in the *Theaetetus*', in Gentzler (1998), 113–36.

MCDOWELL, JOHN (1982), 'Falsehood and not-being in Plato's *Sophist*', in M. Schofield and M. C. Nussbaum (eds.), *Language and Logos* (Cambridge University Press), 115–34.

MCPHERRAN, MARK L. (1985), 'Socratic Piety in the *Euthyphro*', *Journal of the History of Philosophy*, 23: 283–309; repr. in Benson (1992), 220–41.

—— (1995), 'Socratic Piety: In Response to Scott Calef', *Oxford Studies in Ancient Philosophy*, 13: 27–35.

NEHAMAS, ALEXANDER (1985), 'Meno's Paradox and Socrates as a Teacher', *Oxford Studies in Ancient Philosophy*, 3: 1–30; repr. in Benson (1992), 298–316.

—— (1992), 'What did Socrates teach and to whom did he teach it?', *Review of Metaphysics*, 46: 279–306.

OWEN, G. E. L. (1970), 'Plato on Not-Being', in Vlastos (1970), 223–67, and in Owen (1986), 104–37.

PENNER, TERRY (1973), 'The Unity of Virtue', *Philosophical Review*, 82: 35–68; repr. in Benson (1992), 162–84.

—— (1992a), 'What Laches and Nicias Miss—And Whether Socrates Thinks Courage Merely a Part of Virtue', *Ancient Philosophy*, 12: 1–27.

—— (1992b), 'Socrates and the Early Dialogues', in Kraut (1992), 121–69.

PETERSON, SANDRA (1973), 'A Reasonable Self-Predication Premise for the Third Man Argument', *Philosophical Review*, 82: 451–70.

—— (1981), 'The Greatest Difficulty for Plato's Theory of Forms: The Unknowability Argument of *Parmenides* 133c–134c', *Archiv für Geschichte der Philosophie*, 63: 1–16.

SELLARS, WILFRID (1955), 'Vlastos and "The Third Man" ', *Philosophical Review*, 64: 405–37.

SHARVY, RICHARD (1972), '*Euthyphro* 9a–11b', *Nous*, 6: 119–37.

TAYLOR, C. C. W. (1982), 'The End of the *Euthyphro*', *Phronesis*, 27: 109–18.

VALSTOS, GREGORY (1954), 'The Third Man Argument in Plato's *Parmenides*', *Philosophical Review*, 63: 319–49.

—— (1969), 'Plato's "Third Man" Argument (*Parm.* 132A1-B2): Text and Logic', *Philosophical Quarterly*, 19: 289–301.

—— (1983), 'The Socratic Elenchus', *Oxford Studies in Ancient Philosophy*, 1: 27–58.

WENGERT, R. G. (1988), 'The Paradox of the Midwife', *History of Philosophy Quarterly*, 5: 3–10.

WHITE, NICHOLAS P. (1974), 'Inquiry', *Review of Metaphysics*, 28: 289–310.

WIGGINS, DAVID (1970), 'Sentence Meaning, Negation, and Plato's Problem of Non-Being', in Vlastos (1970), 268–303.

INDEX

DATE DUE

DATE DUE			
MAY 29 '01 X			
MAY 1 4 2001			
GAYLORD			PRINTED IN U.S.A.